Contents

PN 81
.R37

Elements of Literary Analysis

EDMUND REISS

Pennsylvania State University

 THE WORLD PUBLISHING COMPANY
CLEVELAND AND NEW YORK

The New World
Language and Linguistics Series

JOSEPH H. FRIEND
General Editor

INDIANA-
PURDUE
WITHDRAWN
LIBRARY

DEC   1973

FORT WAYNE

Published by The World Publishing Company
2231 West 110th Street, Cleveland, Ohio 44102

Published simultaneously in Canada by
Nelson, Foster & Scott Ltd.

First Printing

Copyright © 1967 by Edmund Reiss

All rights reserved. No part of this book may be
reproduced in any form without written permission
from the publisher, except for brief passages
included in a review appearing in a newspaper or
magazine.

Library of Congress Catalog Card Number: 67–14829

Printed in the United States of America

Preface

This short book is intended as a first word, not the last word, of literary criticism. Although it may offer some insights to practicing critics, it is directed at those students approaching literature seriously or formally for the first time. Whereas most introductions to criticism seem to prefer approaching literature in terms of its component parts—plot, character, setting—or its various genres—drama, novel, lyric—I have been most concerned with themes, patterns, and formal techniques. It is fair and probably accurate to say that the present work represents by and large a combination of the approaches offered by New Criticism and archetypal criticism. Although there have been scores of different approaches to literature in the history of criticism and dozens in this century in the English-speaking world alone, many of them seem more concerned with other matters than the work of literature. For example, biographical criticism often tends to neglect the work in favor of its author, folk criticism is likely to be most interested in the folklore itself, psychological criticism is apt to use criticism as a means of promoting Freud or Jung, and sociological criticism may turn out to be an *apologia* for Marx.

Rather than attempt to outline various critical theories or even to follow one to the exclusion of others, I have been interested in trying to point out and demonstrate how, crudely put, one can get at a piece of literature. I have, consequently, used whatever methods happened in my view to be most suitable for the problem or the work at hand. By and large I have found the techniques associated with New Criticism and archetypal criticism—two approaches not necessarily incompatible—to be the most rewarding for understanding both particular works and the generic thing called literature. I have found both approaches necessary because the close analysis of New Criticism is often unable to cope with certain long narratives, and the study of archetypes is frequently not appropriate to certain kinds of lyrics. I have also not hesitated to create my own variations of these approaches even though I may have produced something at which Cleanth Brooks or Northrop Frye might wince. I prefer, however, to say with H. L. Mencken, "The really competent critic must be an empiricist. He must conduct his exploration with whatever means lie within the bounds of his personal limitation. He must produce the effects with whatever tools will work. If pills fail, he gets out his saw. If the saw won't cut, he seizes a club."

I wish to thank New Directions Publishing Corporation for permission to quote Ezra Pound's "In a Station of the Metro"; Doubleday and Company, Inc., for permission to quote translations of a Zen parable and a *haiku* by Taniguchi Buson; and John Balaban and William Packard for permission to quote from their poems. I am also indebted to Priscilla J. Letterman for her fine job of typing from my very rough copy and to my wife Louise for her accurate copy-reading and for her general good humor during the prolonged birth of this book.

Parts of chapters 2, 3, and 6 were prepared in somewhat different form for programs at the Project English Demonstration Center at Western Reserve University and Euclid Central Junior High School, Cleveland, Ohio.

EDMUND REISS

University Park, Pennsylvania
February, 1967

Elements of
Literary Analysis

CHAPTER 1

The Critical Response

In our world today we exist amid a rampage of color, a deluge of sound, and a chaos of words that we ordinarily take for granted. In a world like that of the Middle Ages, however, where the predominant hues were drab, color was exceptional; and people were conscious of brightness wherever it was to be found: flowers in a summer field, water splashing in sunlight, a rainbow shimmering overhead—all made people wonder and marvel. But not all the brightness enjoyed by medieval people was found in nature. Their churches—in many ways the centers of their communities—were likewise filled with vivid hues rivaling and even surpassing those of nature. Not only was the glass of the windows stained so that the light streaming through produced a mixture of strange glows, suggesting something supernatural and miraculous; the church was also filled with brightly colored paintings and statues, and in some the columns, walls, and floor appeared as oceans of swirling colors whose patterns were altered at every moment by the shimmering candlelight. Moreover, the ringing bells and the chanting choir filled the church with a surge of sound that must have acted on the ear as the colors and light did on the eye. All in all the experience of being in church must have been memorable, more so than we can comprehend even when we visit a medieval cathedral.

One must have felt the presence of something above the com-
monplaces of everyday existence, an intimation, as it were, of
the celestial life: one could glimpse the unbelievably bright
heavenly Jerusalem and the celestial harmony of the angels
and the saved.

But how can all of this compare with, say, a modern supermarket? In one of these centers of the modern community we
see aisle after aisle of brightly lit, unbelievable colors. What
in a medieval stained-glass window can rival a large economy-
size box of laundry detergent magnificently orange with purple
letters in a pattern across it? In the supermarket, boxes, bottles,
jars, cans, and bags of all sizes, shapes, and colors produce a
myriad of patterns in their fluorescent brightness that the colors
and shapes in the medieval church could hardly hope to match.
Similarly the hi-fi music piped into the supermarket has a tech-
nical competence and a clarity and variety that the church
choir could not even imagine, much less equal.

We do not, of course, respond to our supermarkets as the
people of the Middle Ages did to their churches, because the
supermarkets are only one manifestation of brightness and
music in our lives. We live in an age of unrivaled brightness,
color, and sound. Our clothing, buildings, automobiles, and
signs only begin to show how omnipresent color and brightness
are to us; and we have difficulty escaping from the sound of
television sets, tape recorders, phonographs, and transistor
radios. The colors of the billboard on the highway more than
rival those of nature, the sounds from our radios drown out
and make irrelevant the sounds of birds and insects, and motion
pictures and television produce a shifting pattern of action
that transcends looking closely at something motionless.

We are, however, so constantly and heavily bombarded by
sounds and colors that many of us are incapable of being
aware of any but the loudest and most vivid, or those that
produce the most discord. It would seem also that of necessity
we shut out some sights and sounds from our consciousness,
apparently to keep our sanity. When we are in the supermarket,

for example, we may not even hear the canned music: we may respond to it subliminally and buy more groceries, but we may not consciously know it is there. It may be said that, although there is more to hear today than ever before, the quality of our hearing is perhaps less than it was five hundred years ago. We may listen and look more than ever, but it would seem that we hear and see less.

So it is with our reading. So much print exists today in the form of all kinds of newspapers, magazines, digests, paperbacks, and hard-cover books—all demanding our attention—that again it is difficult for us even to recognize what is before us, much less understand and evaluate it. We often do not have patience with something whose merits and possible pleasures are not immediately evident and are not of the sort we have come to expect from what we read. We often lack the patience necessary to recognize the subtle and the sublime, and neglect that which may possibly offer us the greatest pleasures and meaning in favor of that which is flashy, easy, and immediately evident. Rock and roll, country music, and old-fashioned pop tunes are alike in that they offer us a simple, uncomplicated experience. Their appeal is only a surface one; furthermore, even though the song may not last, we know we can always replace it with another that is akin to it. The compelling sound of, say, Beethoven is, by and large, for the educated ear; and even though the chances are that this sound will remain compelling far longer than that of popular music, relatively few of us will take the time to understand Beethoven and what he can offer.

Similarly, when we read, we want what is before us to be immediately interesting and understandable. Because there is so much available to read—most of it an insult to the intelligence of anyone over twelve years old—and because there are so many forms of entertainment other than reading, we tend to insist that a book reach out and, as it were, grab us. We do not want to bring ourselves to it or exert any effort for it. Moreover, when we do respond to a story, a poem, a piece

of music, or a painting, the response itself is frequently superficial. To make this clear, we might view our responses as
divided into three kinds. The first kind is what may be termed
the *sensory response*. It occurs when we look at or listen
to something and it may or may not be a conscious response.
The shopper in the supermarket may not have been conscious
of the piped-in music, but a psychologist might argue that,
whether she realized it or not, it came into her ear and affected
her subsequent actions. Rather than buying only a few items,
she may have responded by prolonging her shopping trip. But
even if her actions were not changed by the music and even
if she was not conscious of its presence, her senses still responded to it. Such a response is obviously the most funda-
mental response to a work of art and is so simple that we may
not even want to call it a response. Still, it is one, and the
main difference between it and the response we have when we
put our hand on a hot stove is that the second is the more
noticeable.

To give a better illustration and to develop the idea further,
we may imagine someone wandering through a museum looking at paintings. Over a period of half an hour, this person will
doubtless have *looked at* scores of pictures; he will, in other
words, have had a sensory response to them. But the chances
are that, unless he has an especially trained and appreciative
eye, he will have *seen* relatively few of them. What this means
is that most of the paintings on which his eyes fall do not
mean anything to him and are not able to create an *emotional
response* in him. This second kind of response, which is not
synonymous with *seeing* the painting, depends on more than a
sensory response. Suddenly the stroller's eye may touch upon
one painting out of dozens along a wall, and his eye may rest
there. The painting itself may mean something to him, and
he may not even feel an immediate need to read the card by
it to find out the author or date of the work—details all irrelevant to it as a work of art. The painting itself is significant
to him in its own terms, and he apparently finds both pleasure

and point in looking at it. He is not merely killing time aimlessly casting his eye about him. One sensory response out of many has resulted in an additional response—which may indeed be termed an experience.

We can change the illustration and talk about music we hear or poems we read, but the point is the same. Whenever we have an emotional response, we have felt or intuited something meaningful to us; and when this response occurs, we can focus on it. We can ask, if we are deeply interested in our own psychology, why we have responded as we have, and why to the particular painting, music, or poem. But insofar as these works of art are concerned, such a query is irrelevant. It may have relevance for us, but it should not be thought of as helping us to understand the work at hand. When we look at a work through our response to it, we are committing what W. K. Wimsatt, Jr., and Monroe C. Beardsley have termed the "affective fallacy." Rather than ask, "Why has this work affected me as it has?" we should inquire, "What in this work has caused me to respond as I have?" The emphasis in the two questions is quite different: the first focuses on the person asking the question; the second on the work of art. It is this second question that is the starting point of all real literary criticism.

When we are sufficiently interested in a work of art to ask this, we have arrived at our third response, which may be termed the *aesthetic response*. We have come to it through the emotional response, but now that we are interested in the work of art, we should be interested in it on its own terms. We should now separate ourselves—our personal likes and dislikes—from the work; and we should make an effort to see what it is doing in and of itself, and how, in terms of its artistry—its arrangement of parts—it goes about doing it. It is hardly enough to say that such and such a painting is interesting because it is of, say, a ship. We might like ships and reproductions of them, but ships themselves do not of necessity make interesting paintings. Perhaps the specific subject matter, ships, has made us respond to a painting; but as soon as we are concerned sufficiently about it to see how it works, we have moved from the emotional to the aesthetic response. And when we make this move, the subject, the ship itself, loses whatever special significance it may have had for us. To say this in another way, the painting could be of a cow. When we look at the artistry that created the whole work, we are most interested in the structures on the canvas, the blend of colors, the balance of the shapes, those things that make the painting successful as a work of art. And this artistry will be there whether or not the viewer likes cows.

The aesthetic response thus enables us to see the work of art objectively, that is, apart from our subjective emotional response. Insofar as criticism is concerned, this emotional response must be viewed as a means, not an end. Yet this emotional response is necessary for us to want to get to the aesthetic response and for our aesthetic response to be very meaningful. Our analysis of the work of art would most likely be sterile, lacking real meaning or point, because we have not been able to feel the effect and effectiveness of what we are talking or writing about. If we are not committed to the work at least to the extent of wanting, even needing, to look at it closely, our criticism becomes a chore and can hardly result in any pertinent insights. It is this aesthetic response that produces what may legitimately be called *criticism,* a term that has gone its own way in popular usage and now means something rather different from when it is used in terms of literature and the arts. If in popular usage we say that someone is criticizing an action of ours, we most likely mean that someone has spoken against that action. Criticism in this sense means adverse criticism, whose opposite would be praise. But in terms of art, music, and literature, criticism means analysis—the process, to repeat, of understanding what a work is doing in and of itself and how it is doing it. We may appreciate the work before we analyze it, but real appreciation will come only after we understand its meaning and artistry.

And it must not be thought that analysis or even appreciation is the same as value judgement. Too often when one says that a work is good, he means only that he likes it; and too often the statement "I like this painting because it is good" comes to mean "This painting is good because I like it." Both statements are suspect, and not just because the distinction between them may become blurred. There are many things we like that we cannot really call "good"; and, as far as the second statement is concerned, it is meaningless, even ridiculous, for us to set up our likes and dislikes as the measure of merit. Too often value judgments are really statements of taste, and taste is something that cannot be measured or argued with. One's taste may not agree with someone else's; certain tastes may be fashionable at certain times; one may make a remark that is "in bad taste" at least insofar as certain hearers of the remark are concerned; but taste cannot be wrong or, for that matter, right. Value judgment, like appreciation, is meaningful only as an extracritical response or as one that is relative, not absolute. We may say, for instance, looking at two paintings of ships, that one is more effective than the other, that one is doing more and doing it better than the other; but we can hardly give one a rating of, say, C and the other A. As far as criticism is concerned, such ratings, and all such absolutes, are without meaning and appear at best ridiculous.

To change the illustration to literature, it is hardly adequate or relevant to say, as a student once informed me, that the Big Four of English literature in order of rank are Shakespeare, Milton, Chaucer, and Spenser. I asked him why he thought Milton was better than Chaucer, but he could say nothing. Someone had told him what he repeated to me, and he thought that was the way things were. The idea that someone would ask him to defend his evaluation had never occurred to him. When I continued to prod and asked further why he thought Spenser was any good, what he thought was Chaucer's accomplishment, and even why he thought Shakespeare was better than the others, he floundered more and grew increasingly bewildered. In his mind it was enough to know who the masters of English literature were (though it is moot that those he mentioned are the best writers), he had no desire or thought to understand the writings of these men.

Even in speaking of writings, it is a waste of breath to say that *Hamlet* is "better" than *Paradise Lost* or that the *Canterbury Tales* is "better" than the *Faerie Queene*. The inquiry should be to understand the accomplishment—the strengths and weaknesses—of each of these works; and to do this, one must understand their meaning and artistry. No piece of writing is unfit as a subject of critical inquiry. Some works may reveal more than others because some are richer than others, but none is without significance, because, until we analyze a work, we really do not know what it contains or how rich it is.

It may be further stated that critics are made and not born. The only precondition for literary criticism is a sensitivity to language and a determination to understand what one is reading. The sensitivity is the ability to have an emotional response; the determination is the willingness to take time to understand the work at hand. Some people will never be critics; but if one does not work at analyzing pieces of literature, he cannot possibly know how to criticize. It is not too much of an over-simplification to say that the more one analyzes, the more one is able to analyze. The more one learns how to approach the poem, novel, or play before him, the more he will respond to it and the more meaningful his response will be.

Some people are afraid of analyzing because they view the process as one that takes a work apart and then leaves it in pieces; they see it as similar to a child's irresponsible act of dismantling a clock that has appealed to his curiosity. Works of literature are amazingly hardy, and bad or inadequate analysis can rarely destroy them. All that usually happens is that the person doing the inadequate criticism reveals his own inadequacies. Worthwhile analysis is that detailed examination which appreciates the work in its fullest sense; the criticism that reveals the most about the work may be considered the best criticism. It is the one that comes to grips with all the parts and their functions and sees something approaching the full meaning and art of the work. Whenever we take a work apart and look at it piecemeal, we must do more than study the independent and separate parts. We must also see them in relation to each other and to the whole created by them. The whole in literature is very often more than the sum of the parts, and the work must be seen both in parts and as a whole. We must not disregard any of the parts, because all are in the work and all make it what it is; to miss one is frequently to misunderstand the entire work as well.

We must look closely at the surface of the work at hand, seeing first of all its narrative level, its level of action, and all the parts—plot, characters, and setting, for example—composing it. We must understand these things individually and in relation to each other, and we must see the total effect of the relationships. We must understand how the work is structured. Structure involves not only the arrangement of parts but also such matters as point of view and conflict. *Point of view* as a critical term means the point from which we view the action or scene at hand. We may hear a story as though it happened several years earlier. The author may tell it to us by bringing out various details not known to the people involved in the action. This omniscient author, as he is called, allows us to look at the action from all relevant focal points; with him we not only listen to all the characters' words but also enter their minds and know their every thought.

Or it may be more to a writer's purpose to remove himself from the action and have a character either with a name or called *I*—a narrative *I* that must be viewed as essentially different from the author—report what is happening insofar as he knows it; or perhaps the character will be an actual participant in the action as it is happening at the moment. When such a narrator takes over, the point of view is no longer omniscient, because the character's understanding is limited, incomplete, and perhaps even wrong. In fiction all kinds of points of view are possible, and in many twentieth-century novels and short stories there exists a blend of narrative voices—speaking and thinking, conscious and unconscious—that become as important as (perhaps even more important than) the action being reported. The surface of the work of literature is made up of various levels of consciousness, and the interior voices often enable us to see beyond the exterior voice or the action being referred to.

Even in poems, point of view is an important structuring device, and a narrative poem may be told from a variety of points. In dramatic *monologues,* for example, like those written by Robert Browning, a character is shown speaking in the first person to someone else. Most of these monologues are satiric, for the speaker in them not only reveals what concerns him; through his words he reveals himself to us in a way he may not have realized. Related to the monologue is the *soliloquy.* Whereas monologues present one person speaking aloud—even though we hear only one voice, we know that the speaker is addressing someone else—soliloquies, on the other hand, are verbalized representations of a character's thoughts. They are not to be regarded as spoken aloud or to an audience; we overhear them, as it were. In motion pictures soliloquies are often depicted through a close-up of a person's face while his voice is heard over the sound track. The character's lips are not moving, and we realize immediately that we are hearing his thoughts. But in traditional drama—lacking the mechanical aids of movies—it is customary to have a character walk to one side of the stage and muse aloud. Shakespeare has Iago reveal his evil to us through his soliloquies and allows Hamlet to become more complex through his musings on life and death and the nature of each.

In drama it is difficult to have the variety of points of view possible in novels and short stories, because on the stage there can be no expository or descriptive writing. The words spoken by the characters—their soliloquies, monologues, and dialogues —are the only words that can be in the play (unless a narrator or commentator is used); and we can know only what is revealed through the words and actions of the characters. There may be a variety of voices, both interior and exterior; but, except for such experimental contemporary works as Samuel Beckett's "Krapp's Last Tape"—in the form of a soliloquy or, more precisely, several soliloquies by the same character—plays rely most of all on dialogue. Through the interplay of dialogue showing us statement and counterstatement, question and answer, conflicts are created and resolved.

Conflict is as much a structuring device as point of view. Stories in literature are invariably stories of people or at least involve human emotion. A story about an animal is meaningful either because the animal is presented as a human being in disguise—as in stories of Mickey Mouse or Donald Duck—or because the story is really an appeal to our feelings of sympathy—for example, Bambi. Whenever several characters appear together, we are bound to be conscious of tensions or conflicts between or among them. It is the playing out of these conflicts that in effect creates the narrative level of dramatic and fictional work. Although conflict may be most vividly displayed on the stage, it is a necessary ingredient in any work of literature showing man in relation to his desires, his environment, or his fellows. Even when a work has one character—as in the Beckett play referred to above—conflict is still present, and internal though it may be, at some point it is bound to come to the surface and to our attention.

Sometimes a work of literature will show conflicts that are at the end resolved, or escaped from, or seen as really not conflicts after all. Such works present the familiar happy ending. At other times, however, the conflicts are not resolved; what was wrong at the beginning is still wrong at the end. The work with the happy ending is not inherently superior or inferior to the work ending with a sense of loss and waste. The only ending that can be called bad or inadequate is the one that is not right for the work at hand, the one that represents a wrenching of the given to make it become something it has not been. The ending that does not "solve" all the problems brought up in a work is not necessarily inadequate. It may, in fact, be more adequate than the conclusion that soothes and gives us a sense of security, since it may have made us aware of a moral or ethical problem, an issue relevant to modern life, or a puzzling aspect of human psychology or circumstances. And even if the ending merely makes us face a question or issue we have never faced, it may be more pertinent and effective than the ending that tries to tie up all the loose ends and wrap up the work in a pretty package. We should not be misled into thinking that conflict necessarily deals with contemporary issues or problems. A conflict may be expressed in terms that are particularly meaningful for a certain time or place, but if the work is to be continually meaningful, the conflict must have more than local interest; it must ultimately express something meaningful to men at all times and places.

Two other important elements in literature are style and tone. The two are of necessity related, but *style* may be distinguished as the way in which a piece is written: formal or colloquial, eloquent or plain, intricate or simple. And again no one style is a priori superior to any other. A work may not have many descriptive details on its surface, but it may still be able to say what it wants in the best possible way. Or it may have an abundance of descriptive adjectives and adverbs and a wealth of metaphors and similes; if these are functioning, then this style is right for the work. Certain styles are most fitting for certain subjects and themes. An elegy in memory of someone who died would most probably be serious and formal. But sometimes writers consciously aim at making their styles and their subjects disparate, as Alexander Pope did in his *Rape of the Lock*. In this poem a lover's act of snipping a lock of hair from a girl's head is portrayed as one of the greatest disasters of all times. The extra-serious and formal treatment given this trivial matter makes us aware of how ridiculous the situation is. Pope has produced in this poem a burlesque of the highly serious. He has created from the juxtaposition of style and subject a tone of mockery and satire. Another writer could have done the reverse, taking a serious subject and downgrading it by describing it in a light, bantering style. Again the tone created would be mocking or satiric.

Tone may thus be seen as that which is produced by an author's attitude toward his subject. It is, as has been said, very much related to style; and in popular terminology *tone* and *style* are frequently used interchangeably. But whereas tone often comes about through style, the two are really distinct. It may be said that we are conscious of a writer's attitude when we are aware of the tone he is using, and it is through his style as applied to his subject that he creates a tone.

The *subject* of a work must be distinguished from its *theme,* which may be defined as the concept or attitude revealed through the subject. A subject may be expressed in one word— death, love, nature—but a theme can be described only in a complete thought. A work that has death as its subject may contain the theme that death is essentially unreal or that it is terrible or joyful, sad or happy, the end of all life or the beginning of a new one. Theme is thus the overall concept stated or implied in a work of literature, and, of course, one work can contain many themes.

Although the themes found in a piece of writing may be related to the attitudes of its author, we should never approach a work by asking what its author's intention is. Rather, we should try to understand what the writing itself is doing and should view it as though it were an entity apart from the hand that created it. A work of literature may be likened to a baby. Both are produced by others, but just as the umbilical cord joining child and mother must be cut for the child to have an existence of his own, so that cord joining the work of litera-ture to its author must be severed. We should not be tempted to read a work in terms of what we happen to know about its author and his other works. Rather, we must read it for itself and get its meaning and significance from it and it alone.

We should also realize that an author's intention and his

actual accomplishment may not be the same. If I say that I intend to draw a straight line and end up drawing what everyone else thinks is a curved line, my intention does not matter at all. No one is going to change his view of my line because I insist that I intended it to be straight; he will say it is too bad the intention and the result were not the same. On the other hand, if the straight line I intend does appear to others as a straight line, then my statement of intention is irrelevant. The work reveals what is present and needs no commentary from me. The result is what we are interested in, and in terms of the finished work, intentions are beside the point, as Wimsatt and Beardsley have pointed out with what they call the "intentional fallacy."

If we can show that a certain structure or concept is present in a work of literature and can demonstrate how it functions, it does not matter at all whether the author intended either its being there or its working as we have described. Some people raise the question of how we know that writers put in their works everything we find: "How do we know," they say, "that Shakespeare intended such an interpretation of his play? Suppose he came back from the dead and said, 'But that's not what I meant at all!' Wouldn't that negate everything being said about Shakespeare?" The answer is, not at all. Shakespeare the artist who penned the plays and poems we know is one being; Shakespeare the critic is another. And while Shakespeare the artist is a genius, Shakespeare the critic may be obtuse and naïve. Whenever a writer talks about his own or someone else's writings, he is speaking only as one commentator on the works; and his commentary may be—in fact, is likely to be—less adequate than someone else's.

As existential philosophy has insisted, there is a great difference between knowing and being; and to extend the idea we may say that there is just as great a difference between knowing and doing. The literary artist is involved with his writing, he is creating it, but at the same time he is only the agent of its creation. Going into his writing are various themes, images, and structures that may exist in or be significant to him or his subject; but he is most likely unaware of their presence, much less their significance. To demand that the creative writer "know" what has come from his pen is not only to demand irrelevancies but most probably to bring up something that would get in the way of the creative act.

Writers, composers, and artists are often asked to talk about what they have done, even to tell what certain works mean. But more often than not the comments of these men are, if not gibberish, at least grossly inadequate. The composer Peter Tschaikovsky was once asked to write what he was trying to do in a symphony. After several attempts, he had to give up because he found it impossible to say in the language of words what he had done in the language of music. All he could offer in explanation of what he had done was the symphony itself. Had he been able to express his symphony in terms other than the symphony, it probably would not exist and certainly would not be great art.

So it is with literature. The poem, play, or novel has a meaning and existence of its own; it is independent of its creator and of any attempt—even by its author—to say what it is doing. The creator can do only what the rest of us are doing: look at the work of art from all possible directions, be aware of all its parts and their functions and structures, and understand as much as possible the meanings and significances inherent in and arising from it.

CHAPTER 2

The Nature of Connotation

A man traveling across a field encountered a tiger. He fled, the tiger after him. Coming to a precipice, he caught hold of the root of a wild vine and swung himself down over the edge. The tiger sniffed at him from above. Trembling, the man looked down to where, far below, another tiger was waiting to eat him. Only the vine sustained him.

Two mice, one white and one black, little by little started to gnaw away the vine. The man saw a luscious strawberry near him. Grasping the vine with one hand, he plucked the strawberry with the other. How sweet it tasted![1]

Although actually a Zen Buddhist parable, this short narrative is useful for understanding something of the method of literature, as well as the relationship of the creative imagination to the world of everyday living, which provides most of us with

[1] Paul Reps, ed., *Zen Flesh, Zen Bones* (Tokyo: Charles E. Tuttle Co., Inc.).

our context for comprehending and judging the products of the imagination.

The piece, as transcribed by Nyogen Senzaki and Paul Reps, begins deceptively, in that it appears to be a simple narrative progressing in a way that seems both understandable and logical. Once we accept the first sentence, which wrenches us out of our familiar environment, we enter a world where it is perfectly natural for a man to be chased by tigers that want to eat him. We accept with the first sentence a world apart from the one with which we are familiar, but a world that seems to take its meaning from our world. We are willing to suspend our belief insofar as the details of this particular narrative are concerned, for we know that no matter who or what the characters may be, the story line will parallel one in our "real" world.

But as we follow the adventure of the unfortunate traveler and see his predicament becoming continually worse, the narrative method changes. The camera's eye that directs our attention to various parts of the scene had originally been far away from what it was picturing; thus we saw a man in a field over there, not right in front of us, encounter a tiger. A sense of distance is also suggested by the verb *encountered,* which appears vague and understated; the particularities of the encounter—the way man and tiger met—are never revealed. In fact, the man, the field, and the tiger are all anonymous: we do not know who the man is, what he is doing crossing the field, where the field is, or why the tiger is after him. Still, we accept the statement in all its vagueness and feel that there is no need for particulars.

But then, as the narrative proceeds, the camera's eye moves continually closer to the action, and both action and man become increasingly vivid and meaningful. We see him fleeing, swinging over a cliff, and then trembling as he clutches his vine. Similarly, as the camera moves still closer, we see the tiger sniffing at him; we peer with the man far down to the base of the cliff and are aware of another tiger; we look the situation

over—look particularly at the vine that is his only support—
see and feel the peril he is in. But the man is not to be allowed
even the little security he has. Now that we understand the
hopelessness of the situation, the second paragraph begins a
new action, with the camera's eye moving ever closer, taking in
less but revealing more.

It focuses on two mice, whose particular colors are called
to our attention, and on a single strawberry, which we can see
is luscious. The camera can hardly focus more closely on the
particulars of the scene than it is doing now. With these closeup
shots, the entire development of the narrative changes. We
now see the man, no longer the anonymous and helpless nonen-
tity he has been, initiating an action: he tries to get the strawberry. The emphasis on particulars continues as he is shown
holding the vine with one hand while reaching over with the
other to pluck the berry. The detailed action, which seems
almost in slow motion when contrasted with the vague gen-
eralized action at the beginning of the passage, culminates
finally in the man's eating the berry. We are now so close
to the scene that we even taste with the man how delicious
the fruit is.

But if we were puzzled when the narrative shifted from the
man's response to the tigers to his response to a strawberry, we
are much more so when we find that the line "How sweet it
tasted!" is the final one of the narrative. Something must have
eluded us; the narrative apparently has a beginning and a middle, but where, we wonder, is its end? Not that there is anything wrong with a strawberry tasting sweet, but how can such
a statement be the end of the narrative we have been following?
What has apparently happened in this parable is that one level
of consciousness has replaced another. The original narrative
has made us increasingly aware of the man's impossible predicament, and we feel that with tigers above and below and with
mice chewing away his only support, he does not have much of
a chance to save his life. For us, the pressing question is "What
will happen to him? How can he get away?"

These and like queries are certainly those of the traveler himself until he notices the luscious strawberry. Then a new situation replaces—in his mind, at least—the old one. The most pressing matter becomes how to get that strawberry, how to hold onto the vine and be able to reach it. His success in plucking and eating the berry brings to the narrative a feeling of satisfaction, even of victory, a sense that may be related to Aristotle's idea of catharsis. "But what," asks the frustrated reader, "happened to the traveler?" If the teller of the parable were around, he would most likely respond, "He ate the strawberry." "Yes," answers the reader, more annoyed than ever, "I realize that, but who cares about strawberries! I want to know whether the man got away from the tigers." The teller would then probably reply more ambiguously than ever, "But why do the tigers still matter? After all, he was able to enjoy the strawberry." And, of course, the reader still does not understand.

The reader's frustration exists because of an apparent gap between his consciousness of what is important and the consciousness of the teller of the parable. I used to assign this narrative to students in freshman English for an in-class essay on the first day of the semester, asking them to show what the theme of the narrative was and how this theme was brought out. The experience was usually a terrifying one for most students, who would sit at their desks for more than half the period staring uncomprehendingly at the words before them. The problem of most of them was that they had never experienced anything comparable to the "solution" found in this narrative. When the students finally did write, they would come up with analyses "explaining" the meaning of these few puzzling lines. They would sometimes focus on the two mice— one white and the other black—which they would see as illustrating some sort of statement about the relationships between Caucasians and Negroes. Or the unusual students who did try to say something about the place of the strawberry in the narrative would think that it represented "the false pleasures of the world with which man was deceiving himself." For these students, instead of being properly concerned with the forces about to destroy him, the man could see only what was in front of him. In their scorn they saw the traveler as an escapist, as one who lost his perspective (and their respect) and became ridiculous.

Only after much time and effort could they face the possibility that perhaps the traveler achieved something at the end that made meaningful and perhaps even tolerable his imminent death. Faced with the fact that he must die, the traveler is still able to find meaning and pleasure in his existence—though the students still dwell on his problem. Not so taken up with his predicament that he becomes blind to the beauties and pleasures about him, he is able to enjoy the simple strawberry. He becomes alive here in a way he had not been earlier in the narrative when he existed as the vague anonymous traveler encountering a tiger. The joy the traveler feels as he eats the luscious berry should become the feeling of all readers. The parable insists on this as it ends, not with a gloomy picture of destruction, but with an affirmation of life. It may be most exact to say that death—imminent though it certainly is—has by the end of the narrative become irrelevant.

Perhaps the main reason most people probably have difficulty with this piece is that it does not conform to their preconceived views of how things are. Most of us prefer the comfortable and familiar to that which is strange, and much of the time we do not, or will not, even recognize that which conflicts with our built-in ideas and values. We tend, on the other hand, to examine everything, especially everything we read, in terms of our own consciousness; and rather than accept the unfamiliar for what it is, we often demand that it fit the mold of the accustomed. Few people choose the unfamiliar over the familiar, because of the effort involved in coming to grips with the new. The status quo has its appeals, and few of us would go from even the first-grade to the second-grade reader if we were not pushed. We are lulled and comforted by the predigested and its easy solutions: *Reader's Digest* is more comfortable and easy than, say, *Harper's* or the *Atlantic;* it ties up or cuts off all the loose ends, giving us solutions at all costs.

We cannot imagine the traveler in this narrative if he is any hero worth his salt—that is, a hero like those of, say, movie and television westerns—preferring a strawberry, wild though it may be, to an encounter with a tiger. His facing the situation, accepting it, and then going beyond it seems, to many of us at least, too much like giving up. Picking the strawberry becomes, as the freshmen felt, nothing more than an evasion of the problem. Or rather than recognize as a possible course of action something foreign to our contemporary values and manners, we prefer to read into the work what we want it to mean.

Those who do not really understand literature often remark that, since creative writing is frequently not clear, it may mean something different to each reader. The implication is that every reader brings his own set of preferences and prejudices against which he places the work—which, of necessity, becomes a mirror image of his views. Among museum-goers it is common to see those who stand looking at an abstract painting, not trying to understand what the painting is doing in and of itself, but rather searching to find shapes and forms recognizable to them. So they say, "There, that looks like a hand . . . or is it an eggplant . . . no, I think it's an elephant's ear!" For such viewers, art is disguised reality, and the task of the viewer is to see behind the forms before him and find in the painting the "real" shapes the artist has apparently hidden there. The artistic experience thus becomes comparable to that of the child with a cartoon in which he is told ten faces are hidden. He must look at the picture until he can discover the faces. It is the same, in this wrong view, with literature. Rather than see what is there, certain readers find hidden forms; or if none of the sort expected is there, these readers put them there.

One of the easiest and least rewarding pastimes is to read meanings into works. It is possible, as many have said, to make something mean just about anything we want; but what is much more difficult—and rewarding—is to understand what something means in and of itself. There is a great difference between reading in and taking out, but often, even when we mean well, we confuse the two processes and project meanings without knowing what we are doing—as did the students who read the two mice of the parable in terms of concepts familiar to them in their own lives. Most people have no trouble when asked to understand the stated content, the narrative level, of a story. The trouble comes when they are asked to see that the narrative level is not an end in itself, but the means used by the literary artist to allow his readers to understand certain concepts. Sometimes one hears the accusation directed at writers, "If he had something to say, why didn't he say it more clearly and directly?"—a remark that shows a complete misunderstanding of the nature of literature. The whole problem stems from a failure to comprehend the nature and function of literary language. Some things cannot be said using the ordinary language of everyday experience, just as some things cannot be said using simple sentences or monosyllabic words.

Learning to read usually means learning to recognize groups of letters as verbal units, but reading can hardly stop with mere semantic consciousness, since there are two languages all readers must know. The first is the language of *denotation*. In this language every word has an exact meaning; one may look up the term in a dictionary and find the whole extent of its meaning. As soon as one knows the precise significance of every word in the sentence, he can put the words together and understand the point of the sentence. In denotation one can believe what he reads; there is no ambiguity, or at least there should be none, in the particular meanings of the words. This writing gives us facts; it clarifies rather than confuses, solves rather than challenges.

The second language we must learn is *connotation*. In this language it is not enough to use a dictionary to arrive at a precise meaning for each term, because the terms exist to suggest a wealth of possible meanings. To attempt to find precise meanings for the terms of connotation is to miss the point and deny the value of connotative writing. It is a language that tries to communicate by using verbal principles quite different from those most people are accustomed to using in their daily lives. It is a language that does not strive for direct communication in the ordinary sense of the word. The essential meaning and the apparent meaning are not necessarily the same; and the essential meaning of the sentences of connotation lies not in the particular words of the sentence but in the implications of these words and of their combinations.

To say "When Tom is angry, he frowns" is to state something that no one who knows the meaning—that is, the precise meaning—of each word will have any difficulty comprehending. It is a statement of what may be considered a fact: we have been told something particular about Tom, something we can test and agree on. If someone were to say that the sentence means Tom laughs when he is angry, we should point out that this person did not hear correctly or did not comprehend the words. But with another sentence, "When Tom is angry, he becomes a lion," the matter becomes more complicated. Here we can look up in a dictionary all the words of the sentence, but we still have not necessarily understood the sentence. If we view it literally, or denotatively, we would say that when Tom is angry, he actually turns into a lion, complete with yellow eyes, fangs, claws, fur, and long mane.

This is hardly the meaning of the sentence, which is using a principle of language completely different from that in the first sentence, where Tom was described as frowning. In this second sentence, we are asked to understand that *lion* functions not as a precise descriptive substantive in the comparison being made but as a *symbol,* a term containing several possible meanings. *Lion* is a term that gives a localized, concrete existence to abstract qualities; and in becoming a lion, Tom is really taking on characteristics that have been thought, by our civilization at least, to belong naturally to lions. That is, some possible meanings of *lion* are courageous, strong, fierce, savage, and brutal. We can run the gamut from the good to the bad. What will determine a more narrow range of meanings is the context of the sentence or the tone of voice with which it is uttered, or both. If one admires Tom, the first three connotations will be particularly relevant; if, on the other hand, one is criticizing Tom, the emphasis will probably be on the last two connotations. Still, it is impossible to say precisely *which* connotation is the particular one being called up in the sentence. One-for-one correspondences tend in fact to reduce, if not negate, the symbolic value of a term.

The language of connotation—traditionally found in the form of verse but not necessarily so—is a special language often reserved for situations and subjects too demanding for denotation—traditionally the language of prose. Denotation as prose is the language of the world, the speech of everyday living. Fit for prosaic subjects—the relationship between *prose* and *prosaic* is not accidental—it has limited scope. Most civilizations other than those of the modern Western world have realized this and have reserved for connotation, as for verse, those subjects and insights that cannot be handled by a familiar commonplace language. Denotation is fine for giving us knowledge of facts, but facts are dead, as Alan W. Watts and others have pointed out. If they were not dead, we should not be able to "handle" them. For attaining wisdom, however, for expressing truths and insights beyond the commonplace, one needs connotation and its ambiguities. The user of connotation, the literary artist, was thus combined with the prophet; he was the inspired sayer of truth, literally (as in the Latin term *vates*) the soothsayer. What he spoke or sang of was often a particular kind of truth, one different from that revealed by the ordinary facts of everyday living; and the language he used was an inspired language likewise different from the language of everyday affairs.

Two levels of truth are thus to be distinguished: what we term knowledge and wisdom. Even though the distinction between these has become so blurred that they are most often thought of as synonyms, knowledge may be defined as the truth of facts, of basic familiar events and ideas, and wisdom as something special, something that only an inspired few possess and are able to express. At the beginning of the Middle Ages—the most recent age in the Western world to distinguish between these terms—St. Augustine referred to these as two ways to Truth (*scientia* and *sapientia*). The first, the counterpart to our knowledge, is significantly the root of our word *science* and is the way to truth our society has come more and more to respect. But in St. Augustine's time *scientia* was the lesser of the two ways; *sapientia,* wisdom—that which was the result of insight and inspiration—was far greater. The truths of technology and business are the modern descendents of *scientia,* and those of literature, art, and music are the descendents of *sapientia,* although in our society, literature and the arts are not thought of as giving wisdom.

Whereas in the culture of the West during the Middle Ages as well as in several Eastern cultures, the poet was the voice of his society's values, a voice listened to with respect, even awe, today the literary artist is popularly seen fulfilling the role of entertainer. The concept of two kinds of truth no longer has meaning for us; we tend to accept as true the pragmatic "facts" of life, and literature has become something we read to kill time or to lull ourselves to sleep. Such an attitude has increasingly alienated the serious artist; more often than not he is now apart from and at odds with his society—little wonder when he knows that most people who even bother to read books at all view him as an entertainer, a teller of interesting stories. Such readers, and such a society, are not apt to understand or desire books that demand their full attention and challenge their basic values and prejudices.

While a serious writer may write to make money—few in any profession prefer to starve—the point of his work may be called a reexamination of the familiar. What he is demanding of us, his readers, is that we must confront and understand ourselves and our world; we must see what we are and what the world is and how we exist in it. Or further, as Ralph Waldo Emerson wrote, "We learn nothing rightly until we learn the *symbolical*[2] character of life." We are, however, all too often interested only in what is right before our eyes and in what is undemanding. We like comic strips and simple stories that contain over and over essentially the same characters, the same plots, and the same oversimplified ideas; we turn on the television set to watch movies or plays that use stock situations, images, even words, and that have clichés for solutions and themes; or we watch and listen to sing-along programs that lull us by presenting the old favorites. We continually prefer the simple and the familiar, and in our reading we ask for the same things. Little wonder that we find serious novels and plays —those that are trying to do more than entertain—boring, tedious, and confusing. Still less wonder that we are uncomfortable in the presence of poetry, which does not give us even a story line as a crutch to hold on to, and which is highly ambiguous.

Whereas ambiguity itself is a weakness in denotative writing and a source of confusion to the reader, it is the whole basis of connotation. Still, literary art is obviously more than the creation of ambiguity. Anyone can be ambiguous merely by being vague. For instance, let us examine the following phrase as though it were connotative writing, even as though it were poetry, which may be defined for the time being as the ulti-

---

[2] In his *A Student's Guide to Literary Terms,* James Taaffe defines symbolism as follows:

"Literally, representing one thing by another, especially the device used to represent something abstract, the term itself is probably one of the most ambiguous in the critic's vocabulary. . . . All literature is, in one sense, "symbolic"; that is, in seeking the ideal metaphor with which to give his concept form, the writer selects his language from all possible words, and that language assumes a *symbolic signif-icance.* It creates a world, an atmosphere, and a form which is not a sign of something else, but which actually *is* the something else it represents. Writers in the *symbolic mode* attempt not to find signs to substitute for something else but to create the very thing itself through symbol. . . ."

mate connotative writing, that which is the fullest and most concise expression of the ambiguous. The phrase is

. . . having, not having . . .

Within it are contained most of the major problems of life, the issues that constantly cause conflict among men. The words are certainly ambiguous in that their possible meanings or implications are almost limitless; and the structure of the phrase, with the marks of ellipsis suggesting that the phrase has no beginning or end, emphasizes the ambiguity. But yet this phrase is not poetry, because although the words themselves have what might be termed a built-in ambiguity, this ambiguity is not being used. What is given is merely a statement of ambiguity, not an application of the multiple meanings residing in the phrase. If another line were added to this one, or if, perhaps, a title were placed before the line, the ideas of the phrase might be restricted and given life. It might be said, therefore, that the essence of connotative writing, of poetry, is *controlled ambiguity,* not merely recording symbolism but using it.

It is not difficult to find signs and symbols if we decide to look for them. The common ones are unobtrusively all around us as essential parts of our everyday lives. From paper money, traffic lights, and advertising trademarks to flags and religious objects, they permeate and mark our daily existence. As a character in one of Nathaniel Hawthorne's fictions phrases it, "Everything, you know, has its spiritual meaning, which to the literal meaning is what the soul is to the body." If all signs and symbols were removed from our lives, we would, in effect, stop living. Some objects and terms have a built-in signification. Sometimes the meaning of a particular object is determined by some characteristic of the object itself—as, for example, a bridge signifying something joining two positions. At other times the meaning is something given more or less arbitrarily to the object—as x is understood to stand for the unknown quantity. In most cases, however, the meanings are something that we learn. That is, to the commonplace things representing signs and symbols in our lives, we learn a response that is stereotyped and general and that we then bring to the things. In some instances it may be argued, as it is in Jungian psychology, that a thing will call up in us a response existing within all mankind—a universal archetypal response that is a mark of being human. Light and darkness or white and black, for example, apparently signify good and evil to all people at all times. To these possibly archetypal symbols, our response is as fixed as to those whose meanings we learned.

The objects and terms to which we have a stereotyped, predetermined response may, as they exist in our lives, be called *signs*. When, however, these signs are used in works of art or literature, they generally function as allegorical symbols. The distinction between signs and allegorical symbols is really more complex than this simple differentiation may imply, but since we are here interested in the existence of symbols in literature, it would be irrelevant to examine in detail the nature of signs, a subject studied well by Suzanne Langer, especially in her *Philosophy in a New Key*.

Allegorical symbols may be defined initially as objects or terms containing more meanings than appear on their surfaces—more particularly, meanings that are brought to the objects and terms by the reader as much as by the writer. To say this in another way, the author of a connotative work that uses allegorical symbols is referring to a set of significations preexisting in the world outside his work, a group of meanings with which he knows his audience to be familiar and which he wants them to bring to his work so as to obtain an understanding of it. Allegorical symbols may even be thought of as a kind of literary shorthand where all the author has to do is refer to something everyone knows. Such a method enables him to be concise in the creation of his symbols, to use objects and terms as though they were dehydrated pills to which his readers could add water and cause the pills to become a turkey dinner with all the trimmings. We may even be reminded in this of the story in which a group of people who liked to tell jokes had all their funny stories numbered. Then to tell a joke all one had to do was call out a number; everyone would know what joke was being referred to and would respond with general merriment. The numbers function exactly like allegorical symbols.

A further characteristic of allegorical symbols is that they have no life of their own, no reality apart from their existence in reference to something else. They are apparently concrete manifestations of abstract qualities, which may thus be thought of as more real than the allegorical symbols calling them to mind. Inherent in these symbols is the equal-sign (=) of mathematics. That is, when we come upon one of them, we must immediately translate it into other terms. It exists, in fact, to be translated; and if we fail to make the translation and, instead, regard it as an end in itself, we are missing the point of its existence and mistaking its purpose. The allegorical symbol is like the statue over the courthouse door of a woman draped in the classical manner, carrying in one hand a sword, in the other a pair of scales, with a blindfold over her eyes. All the details of the statue are present to bring out certain characteristics of justice, and taken together they form a certain idea of justice. But certainly the statue is not justice itself. It is merely a representation of justice, and in looking at it we can get an idea of the nature of the abstract concept. The statue has no reality, no existence, of its own; it is present only to take us to a reality away from the object itself.

The object in allegorical symbolism may thus be thought of as less real than what it represents. The object is, as C. S. Lewis has pointed out in his *Allegory of Love,* a cloak thrown over the real, a cloak we must remove to get at the real. The handy thing about this cloak is that it generally contains directions on how to remove it. When we see in a medieval morality play the figure of a fat man riding on a pig, we do not think of ourselves as being in a world of fantasy. Rather, we merely take the object and realize that it is a vivid but oversimplified personification of the sin of gluttony. The figure tells us nothing about what gluttony actually is, any more than the figure of justice defined justice for us. That figure gave us an inkling of various facets of justice; this personification gives a suggestion of the effects of gluttony. By emphasizing the physical effects on human beings, by stressing the grotesquerie and bestiality associated with gluttony, the fat man on the pig suggests to us how we should regard this sin; but we are neither seeing the sin nor getting a real understanding of it.

There exists another form of symbolism that is different from allegory. Because of the inadequacies of critical terminology, this form is often called just symbolism, with no distinction made, initially at least, between it and allegorical symbolism. Perhaps, though it might not readily clarify the matter, we can call this second form *symbolic symbolism*. Although both allegorical and symbolic are based on ambiguity, there are several essential differences between the two forms. Whereas in allegory the given has no existence of its own, in symbolism it has an actual life in its own right, an actual place in the real world as well as in the literary narrative being constructed. Whereas the statue of justice and the personification of gluttony exist merely to take the viewer to the ideas represented by them, the figure of the white whale in Herman Melville's *Moby Dick*, for example, is entirely different. The white whale is initially and actually a whale, not an approximation or representation of abstract ideas. As a whale, the figure of Moby Dick is essential to the narrative level of Melville's novel. Although the figure is obviously more than a whale, it still is literally a whale, and the narrative is literally a whale hunt. We can regard Moby Dick as a whale in a way we could not regard the lion in the metaphor "When Tom is angry, he becomes a lion." There, as we found, if we tried to view the lion as literally a lion, we would be misunderstanding the sentence. But Moby Dick incorporates the literal identification of whale while at the same time being much more than whale.

A further difference between this symbolic whale and the allegorical figures of justice and gluttony is that we cannot find one word to describe the essential nature of Moby Dick. The whale seems to have an ambiguity far beyond that of the other figures, and at the same time the whale contains its own symbolic meanings. That is, we do not bring to Moby Dick an idea of the traditional significance of whales. Whatever meaning Melville's whale has is the result of Melville's creating this meaning; there is no predetermined, stereotyped response to which Melville can merely refer. Thus, of necessity the symbolic is more real than the allegorical, for the writer has to create within the body of his work the meaning of the symbolic. He must have a developed narrative that creates the symbolic object first as real object. Before something can exist symbolically in the second sense of the term, it must first exist. We might even make the assertion that the most symbolic must of necessity be, if not the most realistic, at least highly realistic. When symbolism "fails"—that is, when it elicits no response in the perceptive reader—the symbolism itself is not to be blamed; rather, the vagueness or garbling of the reality of the symbol should be blamed.

The essentially canned or prepackaged nature of the allegorical, as opposed to the symbolic, may be seen in the earlier illustration of connotative writing, "When Tom is angry, he becomes a lion." Here several meanings are possible because of *lion's* allegorical existence outside the sentence. Suppose, however, the sentence had read "When Tom is angry, he becomes a gnu." No longer is the sentence meaningful, because the referent of *gnu* has no built-in symbolism—in our culture at least—as does that of *lion*. If a writer wants to make *gnu* symbolically meaningful, he must take the time to create its values.

Still, something having a predetermined significance may at times function symbolically rather than allegorically. Such a change may take place when the essential significance of a given object or term is altered. Again in *Moby Dick,* for example, Melville has a chapter called "The Whiteness of the Whale," in which he examines the idea of whiteness, generally associated with light and life, with the pure and the good. Melville, however, brings out the frightening possibilities of white as he explores its associations with paleness and with the spectral or ghostly. The "good" qualities suggested by the color still remain, but now additional connotations of "evil" become relevant. The figure of the white whale thus becomes more and more ambiguous, incorporating both good and evil and revealing this ambiguity through a color that usually has a stereotyped meaning. White thus changes from something existing outside Melville's work to something that both takes its meaning from and gives meaning to the work. It furthermore changes from being an equal-sign: it now leads us to a signification and becomes something real in itself that we must reckon with if we are to understand the novel.

Such a use of what may be termed opposing symbolic values in one object is nothing new to literature. In the Middle Ages, for example, symbols characteristically contained two sets of meanings, each the opposite of the other. The figure of the lion stood both for Christ, the lion that becomes the lamb, and for the devil, the raging lion that seeks to destroy man. Although both meanings were possible each time the term *lion* was used, the context of the term determined the signification relevant for that moment. Of course, at any moment both sets of signification could be relevant. This process represents, in effect, a combination of the allegorical and the symbolic. The object has built-in meanings that are used in the narrative not as ends in themselves but as the basis for creating still other meanings.

It may also be seen that the symbolic not only has a greater reality than the allegorical but also is real in itself. Whereas the allegorical was described as being like a cloak we must remove to get at the essentially real, the symbolic itself is the essentially and existentially real. The statue of the blindfolded woman holding sword and scales and the figure of the fat man on the pig are disguises which may be removed. In these the tangible, the flesh and blood, is a mirror image of a greater reality than is found in the objects themselves. This greater reality is, as has been stated, the ideas of justice and gluttony, which may be separated from the objects that represent them. We go through the objects to get at the ideas, but once there we are detached from the objects, which consequently lose their reality.

It is impossible, however, to separate the idea represented by Moby Dick from the figure of Moby Dick, because connotation after connotation pulsates from him. He demonstrates vividly Samuel Taylor Coleridge's idea that symbolism shapes new wholes and hence is esemplastic. Even if we say that the white whale represents the ambiguous combination of good and evil in the world, we must see this combination in terms of him. We cannot cut any cord joining whale to meanings of whale. Meanings derive from him, but he also derives from the meanings; they exist because of him, but he also exists because of them. Each constantly creates and nourishes the other, and if we are going to understand Melville's novel, we must understand symbol not only as product but also as process, as something constantly going on. We get from Moby Dick an idea of what Thomas Carlyle meant when he said, "In the symbol the Infinite is made to blend itself with the Finite, to stand visible and, as it were, attainable there."

We are, by and large, more comfortable with the allegorical than with the symbolic. The allegorical is easily encompassed by our minds and easily translated into terms with which we feel familiar and comfortable, but the symbolic defies encompassing and translation. It must be seen in all its ambiguity or it is not really seen at all. To say that the figure of Moby Dick stands for this or that is no way to proceed. We must first see what Moby Dick is—the difference between *is* and *stands for* is essential—and we do this by reading Melville's narrative and realizing that our view of the white whale comes from this narrative. We must neither neglect nor oversimplify any detail. Too often we look for one-for-one correspondences in connotative writing, and end up missing the whole point.

Symbolic meanings are like waves rolling in from the ocean to the shore. If, at any given moment, we are asked to point to a certain wave, say the tenth wave out from shore, we can

only point in the general direction, perhaps fifty feet from
shore, where the wave might be. We certainly cannot point to
any specific wave and say that it is the tenth wave, because
as we point the waves change. Still, whereas we cannot be precise about this tenth wave, we can still be wrong. If we point
to a wave then hitting shore or to a wave a mile out at sea, we
are hardly pointing to what is the tenth wave at that particular
moment.

In a similar manner it is possible to be wrong about the
meaning of a symbol. Too many people think that the interpretation of symbols is a no-man's-land or, more precisely, an
everyman's land where everyone's view is as good as everyone
else's, where, in effect, it is impossible to be wrong. The erro-
neous premise in such an attitude seems to be that everyone
is thinking in terms of what the symbol means *to him*. Such a
question would be interesting if we were interpreting the reader,
but since we apparently want to understand the work of literature, the question should be "What does the symbol mean
in the work itself?" There is a great difference, as was mentioned earlier, between reading things into a work of literary
art and understanding what is present in it. Symbols, as Emerson wrote, compel the reader to share in the discovery; they
rouse him to escape from "all frozen limitations of dogma to
an ever-fresh awareness of the multiple facets of truth."

One interesting way of examining symbolic language is to
look at nursery rhymes. We may view them in terms of *topical
allegory*—that is, what they may have meant as commentaries
on the age in which they were produced, or what their authors
intended to satirize in them; but topical allegory is, as far as
literary criticism is concerned, a profitless subject. Even when
it really does exist, it does not help our understanding of what
a work of literature essentially means or of how it functions.
If we know Jonathan Swift's *Gulliver's Travels* simply as a commentary on eighteenth-century English politics, we have hardly
understood the meaning of the work which transcends both
its author and the age in which it was produced. Likewise

with nursery rhymes, no matter what topical allegory may be present, there are still meanings that are the reason for the rhymes' continuing existence.

But what are we to do with such a piece as "Mary had a little lamb"? It tells a story, albeit a rather insipid one, but nothing is really done with the story. We might try to view this little rhyme symbolically, as perhaps an allegory of the life of Christ, Mary being the virgin who has the lamb, Jesus. In the lamb's going to school we have Christ in the temple with the learned men; in the teacher's attitude toward the lamb we can have the Pharisees' response to Christ. We can go on and on with this interpretation, but while it may be entertaining, it has little to do with the verses at hand. As was said, there is a difference between reading a significance into something and understanding the thing in and for itself. This allegorical interpretation of "Mary had a little lamb" is a projection of one point of view onto the poem. In effect it translates the poem into other terms that tend to give it more significance than it actually has. As we make this interpretation, we bring the poem into our familiar world; but such an effort is not the business of criticism. As best we can, we must view literature apart from our own premises and prejudices.

No matter what "Mary had a little lamb" may once have meant, the verse means little today except a pleasant series of sounds and rhythms. We might say that the narrative level seems to be the whole meaning of the poem. Of a different sort is another nursery rhyme, "Hey, diddle, diddle, the cat and the fiddle." Here we are in the presence of symbolic language, of the creation and patterning of ambiguity:

> Hey, diddle, diddle,
> The cat and the fiddle,
> The cow jumped over the moon.
> The little dog laughed
> To see such sport,
> And the dish ran away with the spoon.

We are not able to reduce these words to familiar meanings. They are ambiguous and inexplicable, but yet they are not gibberish. There is something compelling about the combination of sound, rhythm, and images that makes this nursery rhyme a far more poetic piece of writing than the prosaic "Mary had a little lamb."

In like manner Lewis Carroll's "Jabberwocky" is more than a verbal curiosity or a piece of whimsy having no essential seriousness:

> 'Twas brillig, and the slithy toves
> Did gyre and gimble in the wabe:
> All mimsy were the borogoves,
> And the mome raths outgrabe.

Without thinking rationally about the verse, we know what the words are doing and what the lines are saying. We may not know what it all "means," but that is really beside the point. Once we accept the world of symbolic language as something whole and real in itself, our frames of reference are no longer the basis for our understanding, and it is important that we do not project them into this world. The fact that we cannot transfer connotative language into our own everyday denotative language should not disturb us. If we could, the poem's language would not be connotative. After all, to paraphrase Robert Frost, poetry is what cannot be translated. Poetry is the ambiguity at the center of the work, and to put connotative into denotative language is at least as hard as translating a lyric from one tongue into another or putting a piece of music into words.

CHAPTER *3*

Levels of Meaning

Connotative language has been described as poetry and as being chiefly in the form of verse, but it is important to recognize that this language also exists in prose, as a brief illustration from Stephen Crane's short story "The Open Boat" will show. Whereas I intend primarily to use it to show something of the nature and function of connotation, I must of necessity also point out the artistic control being exercised here and the relationship between this artistic control and the meaning of the piece:

> None of them knew the color of the sky. Their eyes glanced level, and were fastened upon the waves that swept toward them. These waves were of the hue of slate, save for the tops, which were of foaming white, and all the men knew the colors of the sea. The horizon narrowed and widened, and dipped and rose, and at all times its edge was jagged with waves that seemed to thrust up in points like rocks.
>
> Many a man ought to have a bathtub larger than the boat which here rode upon the sea. These waves were most wrongfully and barbarously abrupt and tall, and each froth-top was a problem in small-boat navigation.

These are the first two paragraphs of a story about four ship-
wrecked men, but rather than give us explicit background in-
formation, the writer is most concerned with creating a certain
feeling or atmosphere which carries along the narrative and
which, finally, gives meaning to the total effort of the story.

When we read the first sentence, "None of them knew the
color of the sky," we do not yet know what is happening.
There is, as a consequence, something mysterious in the vagueness, but this opening is quite different from the vague one of
the parable of the traveler and the tigers. There the story
began with a general occurrence that became progressively more
vivid and particular. Here, on the other hand, we begin *in
medias res,* right in the middle of the action. We have come
upon an action that has apparently been going on for some
time and that is part of an even larger set of events which
includes the shipwreck. But as our attention is directed by the
writer, it focuses on the men in the lifeboat and on their
responses to what is happening to them. The first sentence
does not help us understand what is occurring; it is, rather, a
puzzling statement. Our response to it might justifiably be,
"Why didn't they know the color of the sky?"—a question
answered in the second sentence. It is our response to the
writing that carries the writing along, and it is the writing that
creates further responses in us.

When we find that the men's eyes are "fastened upon the
waves that swept toward them," we understand something of
their tension, determination, weariness, and trouble. Now, for
the rest of the paragraph, we see everything through the eyes
of these men as though we were in the boat experiencing and
feeling with them. Thus we fix our gazes on the waves which,
almost alive, are sweeping toward the boat and which are "of
the hue of slate," that is, dark or gray. "Why," one might ask,
"didn't the writer simply say the waves were gray? Why did
he have to beat about the bush?" The answer is obvious. To
say that they are "of the hue of slate" is to show something
of their color but also to suggest something desolate, barren,

and unhospitable. The effect would have been entirely different had Crane said the waves were like gray silk. Then the waves would have appeared as gentle, pleasant, and generally enjoyable; their threatening characteristics would have vanished. But "the hue of slate" makes them hard, uncomfortable, and threatening.

A color contrast is also made between these dark rocklike waves and their "foaming white" tops. But the texture of the foam is misleading and ironically in contrast with the slatelike texture of the water. Furthermore, all the men know the reality of their environment: all of them "knew the colors of the sea" ironically contrasts with the first sentence and emphasizes even further their struggle. The slate-gray waves with white tops are like mountain peaks covered with snow, as the last sentence of this paragraph makes clear. As we look out of the boat, these waves fill up the horizon with continual jagged mountains— "waves that seemed to thrust up in points like rocks." There has been a progression in the paragraph: with the developing image the waves become harsher and more threatening until, with the combination of metaphor and simile at the end, there is nothing more to be said about them. Anything else would become an overstatement, and, likewise, constant restatement of the trouble would be superfluous.

Consequently, in the second paragraph the nature of the language and tone changes although it still carries the narrative along with it. Only now are we told explicitly that we have been looking at a boat, although in the first paragraph when we saw the horizon narrow and widen and felt it dip and rise, we experienced the movement of a boat. But now we are no longer in the boat; we are, rather, apart from it listening to the narrator tell us about the scene before our eyes. Through his connotative language in the first paragraph, Crane has created his setting and his conflict—man versus nature—and further made us feel the helplessness of his characters. In the second paragraph the language seems more denotative than connotative. The one exception is the term *bathtub*. Crane does not make an explicit comparison between it and the boat, but through using it he does make us conscious of several relevant matters. Most obviously, we see that the boat is small; it also apparently wallows helplessly in the sea, unsteerable. But still further, in using *bathtub,* something to contain water, Crane has made us aware of the danger the men are in of sinking. With the hint that the boat is taking in much of the sea around it, he makes us see even more the helplessness of the survivors in the boat.

There is also something humorous—incongruously humorous—about this second paragraph. The narrator is making a joke of sorts in the first sentence, and the polite, somewhat flowery language of the second sentence seems out of place both with the plain language of the first paragraph and with the situation itself. To call the waves "most wrongfully and barbarously abrupt and tall" is to bring in the language of polite society, to be emphatic and to negate the emphasis at the same time. No one in the boat would look out at the sea and say, "What wrongfully tall waves these are!" The situation calls for language of another sort, but by using this kind here, Crane insures our awareness of the irony of the situation and of the ironic view of life that permeates and develops in the story that follows.

Before looking further at the nature of meaning in literature, it will be helpful to consider an illustration used by Northrop Frye in his *Anatomy of Criticism.* Frye points out that there are at least three ways of looking at a work of art, say, for purposes of illustration, a painting. If the painting is hanging on the wall, we may stand back from it and describe what its content, its subject is. This would be a description of what may be termed the story in the painting and would correspond to the narrative level in a work of literature. We can then move up to the painting, look at it very closely, and study the techniques and methods used in it. In such a study we would be concerned with the function of and relationship between every single brushstroke, every line, and every color in the painting. This would be a kind of criticism comparable to the one just given of the beginning of Crane's "The Open Boat."

Finally we can step far back from the painting and see the work in terms of the overall patterns that make it up and that are found in other paintings. In this third approach, which Frye has termed *archetypal criticism,* we are concerned with the ultimate and universal themes of the work. We recognize the narrative and its particular themes, we study the methods and uses of connotative language in the work, but finally we look at the meanings that exist beyond the artist's intention, perhaps even beyond his particular time and place. All these ways of viewing the work of art are essential—as is any that adds to our understanding—but it would be well to pause here before the idea of the archetypal.

The patterns forming a particular piece of literature that link it to other literary works may be thought of as the underlying and overall themes of the work. Many works have particular significances relevant to the age of their composition. For instance, a writer may have had a particular war in mind when he wrote against war, but the particular war is only his vehicle. It provides him with an efficient cause for his ideas, but these go beyond his particular intention and subject—or at least they must do so if his writing is to have more than local significance. And if a work is to transcend its particular time and place and have meaning and relevance to all people at all times and places, it must be more than well written—it must have a meaning or meanings that are above or beyond the particular. Most pieces of writing have particular meanings, but only those that go from the immediate and the particular to the universal can be properly termed literature. Some literature aims at the universal without using the immediate and particular as its means, but this kind will be examined later.

When we were examining *Moby Dick* earlier, we were looking at a figure, the white whale, that through Melville's artistry, has universal significance; we may even see it as an archetypal figure. In this novel, whales, whale hunts, American sailors, and the nineteenth century, for instance, are all important to the surface; but this surface is the book's narrative level, and all these things, insofar as they exist as entities in their own right, are ultimately superfluous to the final meanings and significances. They are the means of making the symbols work and as such are necessary parts of the book, but they must be seen as means and not ends. We must go from them to the connotations, the universal themes, that give the novel its continual relevance. It is not easy, however, either to go this way or to understand the various levels of meaning existing within and beyond the work.

To approach these problems, let us take three illustrations and examine them in relation to each other. Such a procedure will help us to understand how levels of meaning exist and also something of how the principles of archetypal criticism work. Let us take Homer's *Odyssey*, Samuel Taylor Coleridge's *The Rime of the Ancient Mariner*, and the comic strip Popeye. One can easily sense the differences among these narratives, but one may also view them as having several traits in common. Like *Moby Dick* on the narrative level, all three are sea stories; at least all center around a hero who is a seaman. Moreover, the hero is in all cases a man who has had wondrous experiences: he has entered the realm of the supernatural, beyond the ken of mortal man. In the case of Odysseus he has stood against Poseidon, god of the sea, against natural disasters like storms and shipwrecks, and against temptresses like Circe and monsters like Polyphemus the Cyclops. Similarly, the Ancient Mariner has experienced the silent sea, which was alive, and he has seen Death and Life-in-Death playing at dice for him. Popeye the Sailor Man has stood up against the Sea Hag and other strange and grotesque figures. In many respects, then, these works may be seen as having much in common on the narrative level; the plots are in many ways the same, as are the characters and the settings.

It is difficult, however, to use such standard aids as plot, character, and setting to help understand these works more than superficially. I suggest that the best way of examining them is in terms of meaning—that is, to see what each work is doing; how it uses the particular, the allegorical, and the symbolic; and to see what are the ultimate theme patterns appearing and working in each.

Hardly anyone would deny that the episodes of Popeye exist primarily on the narrative level: whatever meaning they have seems to be in terms of the story itself. The narratives of Popeye have, in other words, no existence beyond that which is stated. If any ultimate or universal themes are to be found in them, they probably take the form of the explicit moral presented in all the episodes, the meaning that in a sense tends to unify all the various narratives centering around Popeye. This explicit moral is the direction to be healthy and strong, "Eat spinach!" But at the same time, there is no real relationship between the adventures of Popeye and the "Eat spinach" moral. Whereas the *raison d'être* of the adventures seems to be to get to spinach, we all realize that the "Eat spinach" moral is an after-the-fact intrusion, a kind of commercial dragged into the story and one that is really irrelevant to it. After all, the whole idea of the "moral" in literature may be defined as an after-the-fact and individual projection or application of a theme, and generally the moral is quite different from the theme of the work.

In reacting to the narrative of Popeye, one must suspend belief, but this is not difficult to do. The reader finds himself in a world where everything is simpler than it is in his real world. All emotions and meanings are stated, nothing is implied, and one does not have to worry either about cause and effect or about the existence of logical connections between events. Things tend to happen without order or point; they follow a pattern of ever-increasing action but develop no rationale. This world of Popeye could be frightening were it not for the existence of Popeye himself, who acts as the organizing principle of the universe. Popeye is simple, uncomplicated strength. In him problems of moral or ethical values lose their reality

and their importance. Popeye endures until at some point the
can of spinach is thrown down his throat, and then, flexing
his muscles, he conquers the evil forces in the world. With
simple strength he batters down giants and monsters representing the malevolent forces against which man is generally helpless. But although this world of Popeye is filled with fantastic
monsters, the basis of the world is that of the familiar middle-
class American home. The props in this world are such harm-
less and cherished ones as babies—Swee'pea; hamburgers—
Wimpy; and a kind of simple, uncomplicated love between
Popeye and Olive Oyl. This love is unfeeling, even emasculated;
and, ironically, it must be such if it is to be a part of the life
of the rough-and-ready sailor man.

Even though the stories of Popeye exist completely on the
narrative level, and even though the actions and episodes do
not have any symbolic or allegorical significations, the stories
do rise above the particular and the local. They do apparently
contain themes and patterns that are universal, archetypal, and
mythic. Popeye himself represents a wish fulfillment, and as
such may be seen as a kind of folk hero comparable to Davey
Crockett, Paul Bunyan, Robin Hood, or Batman. Stories about
such heroes have always had tremendous interest, especially
for immature minds, in that they tend to dramatize the solving
of problems that may be affecting the lives of the readers.
Just the idea of man's living in a hostile universe is frightening,
but in something like Popeye's narratives the fear is diminished
because the threat is reduced to something tangible. The human
is elevated to something mighty in Popeye, and the solution
comes as a matter of course.

Because we are not really worried about what is going to
happen, the world seen in Popeye's adventures may be ultimately viewed as a comic one, not humorous, but comic in the
sense of showing a view of life based on an abiding faith in
the outcome of human endeavor. Even though there appear
what may seem to be hardships, these hardships represent not a
norm against which man acts but aberrations from a norm.
Man will ultimately prevail, everything will turn out for the

best; God's in his heaven, all's right with the world; and this is the best of all possible worlds. This meaning of *comic* is, of course, that found in the term *comic strips* or *comics*. The stories of Popeye deal with the great archetypal themes of literature but handle these in such a way as to reduce them. The happy ending becomes more important than the act of man's struggle. The intrusion of spinach makes everything appear even more simple. It is implied that if one eats spinach as Mother wishes, one may be like Popeye too, and all one's troubles will vanish as a consequence.

Of course, this kind of narrative may be termed escape literature; that is, through reducing the issues, the literature implies such an easy solution that it can lull one, not necessarily into believing in its solution, but into becoming addicted to facile solutions like the one it presents. One can awaken in the morning and be soothed by Popeye and his friends at the breakfast table. One can return home after a hard day's work, and there Popeye will be, ready to soothe again, ready to be a soporific. After confronting a frightening world, one can always come to Popeye and find that things once again seem serene and secure.

The Rime of the Ancient Mariner works somewhat differently. Here the narrative level is not particular, local, or familiar. To be precise, the work is put in a frame that is this world. In it the Ancient Mariner fixes his eye on a wedding guest and tells his story in spite of the fact that the church bells have begun to ring for the wedding and the wedding guest wants to be off. But the tale that the Mariner tells is the real narrative level of the poem, and, as it proceeds, the normal human world, along with the particular scene of the wedding guest talking to the Mariner, tends to fade from the reader's consciousness. The figure of the wedding guest appears a few more times in the course of the narrative as he interrupts the Mariner's story with expressions of his fear of the Mariner and of what the Mariner is saying to him. But such expressions function to highlight the unreality of the tale.

What happens is that the real narrative level of *The Rime*

of the Ancient Mariner becomes the world of the Mariner's adventures, and this world of ours appears as an allegorical dreamworld. We soon leave the waking human world and move into a world that is not make-believe but real in the sense that it is at the heart of life. But it is a strange, unhuman world, in which things can be reproduced and understood only as shadow shapes. It is a world that at its heart may be called life-in-death, where external appearance has no literal meaning of its own and where the concept of the concrete loses significance. We realize that everything must be seen as suggesting essences beyond or within our world. Even such familiar things as the sun and the sea take on new guises. The Ancient Mariner's ship becomes a strange floating tomb, and his dead shipmates who have fastened their accusing eyes on him become shells filled by spirits from a world beyond the human.

This world of Coleridge's poem is one beyond hamburgers and spinach. Love itself is quite different from what was seen in Popeye's stories by way of the simple, sterile Popeye–Olive Oyl relationship. Now it is an important force holding together all of creation, all of the spiritual and physical world, in a harmonious bond. By killing the albatross the Ancient Mariner violates this power of love. By agreeing that the bird was evil and the Mariner's action of killing it good, his shipmates become accessories after the fact. It is only when the Ancient Mariner unconsciously blesses the water snakes, creatures which seem to be strange and apart from him, that his return to life—that is, to the life of our waking world—begins. He now has recognized, intuitively as it were, the bond of love that joins everything together.

This world of the Ancient Mariner is one in which Popeye would be an impotent and superfluous figure. Popeye might bellow and bluster, flex his muscles and swing his fists, even eat his spinach; but it would all be to no avail. His physical strength would change nothing in the world of the Ancient Mariner, for what is important in Coleridge's poem is not man's physical prowess but his spiritual or inner strength, especially a quality that might be termed "pureness." Whereas Popeye's adventures test the hero in terms of his external strength, *The Rime of the Ancient Mariner* tests the chosen hero in terms of what might be called his inner goodness. To be precise, the Popeye stories do not actually advocate strength; rather, they present strength as the result of, or reward for, eating spinach. But Coleridge's poem puts forward the concept of goodness and is in effect an analysis of the human situation showing the necessity of goodness.

The sea is not used in this poem as a setting for mere adventure, and the Mariner does not appear as the personification of the heroic adventurer. He is, in fact, a weak man in many respects, hardly an ideal or wish-fulfillment figure at all. He is not the victorious hero who knocks down the forces of evil before him. He is more like a victim, and as such he is something of an embarrassment to readers of the poem. The Mariner shows the thoughtless irresponsibility of man, and his story is not something to soothe, entertain, or act as a soporific for the reader. It is something disturbing, and most readers would probably prefer to join the wedding guest and go off to the feasts, the happy events and diversions found in the world. Most readers, we may say, *are* the wedding guest. If the Ancient Mariner can catch their eye and hold them while he tells his story, their view of life may change: they may acquire a consciousness of real problems and of their own inadequacy. The comic view of life found in Popeye is replaced in *The Rime of the Ancient Mariner* by a view that is somber and not at all comfortable. God may be in his heaven, but all is not right with the world, and this world is hardly the best of all possible ones.

In many ways the view of life presented by Coleridge may be termed *tragic*. Many people tend to think of tragedy as the opposite of comedy, but such a view is a misleading simplification. In tragedy we witness an individual struggling to face and come to terms with what is before him. It is not that he must beat it or knock it down with his fists, as does Popeye.

Rather, the important thing is what the facing, the act of confrontation, does to him. If there is a development of consciousness within him, it really does not matter whether he wins or loses, whether he beats down his opponent or is destroyed by him—as in the parable of the traveler and the tigers it did not ultimately matter whether or how he died. The tragic hero may be destroyed but he is not defeated.

Because tragedy focuses on the struggle made by the individual, its scope is much narrower than that of comedy. Tragedy is not really concerned with whether all is right with the world. The tragic work may conclude "happily," but this happy ending is not because the main character has defeated his opponent; it is, rather, because he has gained and developed from the struggle. The struggle has then been justified; even if it results in death, the new consciousness supersedes the death and the struggle. That form of literature which ends on a note of waste may be termed ironic. In irony the ultimate feeling is one of overpowering desolation, a sense that all has been in vain. This is very different from both tragedy and comedy, as will be discussed in detail later. But at this point we may think of *Moby Dick* as an illustration of a work containing the ironic view of life.

In *The Rime of the Ancient Mariner,* the old Mariner does gain in understanding and does change his way of life. After his terrible voyage he is no longer a happy-go-lucky, irresponsible man shooting arrows at albatrosses; he becomes a thoughtful, even brooding figure who has come face to face with the ultimate questions of life and with a supernatural world beyond the normal and the familiar. It is, however, superficial to talk about whether the poem ends happily or successfully. The poet has taken the reader into the unknown and has showed him something of life. Neither Coleridge nor the Ancient Mariner has solved the problems of life; we do not have a feeling of finality or completeness when we finish the poem. Whereas in Popeye it might be possible to say "Eat spinach and all will be well," one cannot understand *The Rime of the Ancient Mariner* by saying "Don't kill albatrosses" or "Be kind to dumb animals." This is to reduce the philosophical content and the universal meanings of the work to a kind of popular didactic statement of morals. In Popeye such a moral or direction might try to give meaning to the narrative level. But in Coleridge's poem, such a moral acts to reduce the narrative level and the connotations it has.

Some readers of the poem attempt to make this moral the entire meaning, and, to be sure, such a restricted meaning does make the poem easier to grasp and respond to. With such a meaning one can "handle" the poem, but such a meaning also emasculates it, reducing it to the level of familiar, everyday life. Rather than approaching the ultimate significations of the work, such an interpretation tends to cut down the work to fit it in our hands and to make us comfortable. Still, it may not be entirely the reader's fault if he tries to reduce *The Rime of the Ancient Mariner* to a didactic assertion of popular sentiments, because Coleridge has written his poem as an allegory and with allegory, as we have seen, it is necessary to make correspondences. We must see the content not as something having a reality of its own but as an equal-sign, or a series of equal-signs, leading to something else. Similarly, one might question the effectiveness of such an allegorical presentation in making the reader respond to the ideas of the work. The reader may understand the fact of the allegory, he may even understand its meaning; but he often has a difficult time responding to it or to the ideas covered up by it because he realizes that it exists not as a fact but as an analogy, even an illustration, of something else.

The *Odyssey* of Homer combines in many ways the methods seen in the popular narrative of Popeye and the allegory of the *Ancient Mariner*. It emphasizes both the world of phenomena and that of noumena (the bases of phenomena, meaning not capable of being sensed but discernible by reasoning) and may consequently be seen not only as a fuller or more complete work of art than the others but also as containing meanings that have appeared in the other two works in what may be termed a fragmented state. The *Odyssey* presents a hero who is both a man of strength and a man of spirit, and on its narrative level it tests this hero's strength and intelligence. Its narrative level, moreover, combines our familiar world and the shadow world of the supernatural. There appear familiar feelings and emotions, familiar concepts of love, for instance; but there also exists the other world of noumena which, by threatening Odysseus, acts as a proving ground for him in his inner development. We see the ogres, the monsters—the Cyclopes, the Lestrygonians, Scylla and Charybdis—all creatures more frightening than the Sea Hag or others of her ilk in the stories of Popeye. We also see temptations in the forms of the Cattle of the Sun and the seductresses Circe, Calypso, and the Sirens. Moreover, Poseidon, powerful god of the sea, has a reality far beyond that found in Death or Life-in-Death in the *Ancient Mariner*.

In many ways the world of Coleridge's poem is a dream, a nightmare; but at the end we are back to the waking world of sunlight and church bells, back in "our own countree," and the nightmare has passed. In the *Odyssey,* on the other hand, the matter is somewhat different. It is not merely that we must endure the nightmare; by and large, the narrative level of this epic does not give the dreamlike impression of *The Rime of the Ancient Mariner.* In the *Odyssey* the supernatural world is as real as the natural world. Here the supernatural world of noumena, the world beyond or within this one, is presented in a way that can properly be termed symbolic. Polyphemus, the Cyclops, is as real as Moby Dick; and he suggests the bestiality that crafty Odysseus must overcome before he can arrive home, defeat the suitors, and regain his wife and kingdom. It is the narrative level of the *Odyssey* that makes Polyphemus symbolically meaningful. Similarly, it is the narrative level that shows Circe and Calypso representing the claims of the flesh, the passion that must likewise be overcome by the hero. By having these creatures exist as real entities, Homer avoids the kind of allegory seen in Coleridge's poem. Moreover, Homer avoids the didacticism found in a work that states abstract ideas rather than suggesting them through concrete objects.

Still, though Polyphemus and Circe may be as real as Moby Dick, they are not completely or ultimately symbolic. They are more like the figure of Queequeg in Melville's novel. We can see and describe fairly easily what they represent, but not so with the white whale or Ahab in *Moby Dick,* and not so with Odysseus, the hero of the *Odyssey.* Odysseus is a real man, not a folk ideal like Popeye. But he is also a representative of man, not simply conquering hero on the one hand or victim on the other. Through him man may make the journey out of our world of reality into one beyond this and then finally return home. But everything is not no simple or concise or worked out as in *The Rime of the Ancient Mariner.* In the *Odyssey* we focus our attention on Odysseus' struggles. Aided by the Greek personification of wisdom, he is seen as a man achieving his ends not through brute physical force but through inner nobility, inner strength, and wisdom. To say it in another way, Odysseus is tested and proved in two areas, in the external world of the body, the outward world of human affairs—which is the world we do not see in the *Ancient Mariner*—and in the internal world of the self. Odysseus' voyage is both in the actual physical world and within the self. It is, in fact, only after Odysseus descends to the Underworld and returns—is born again—that he is the new man, the hero who can return to his home in Ithaca.

One may even say that Odysseus ultimately succeeds in his journey because he is human, not a shadow shape. One cannot speak meaningfully about the humanness of Popeye, and in Coleridge's poem, humanness is seen as weakness. But in the *Odyssey* humanness is depicted as both the given and the ideal. No attempt is made in the poem either to glorify or to denigrate human existence and human life. In these terms a significant scene in the *Odyssey* occurs when Calypso offers Odysseus immortality. What her offer means is that the hero has the chance to be more than human, to go beyond man and his frustrations and problems. If Odysseus were immortal, he would no longer be concerned with the questions of justifying the ways of man and of the world to himself. He would not have to worry about the difficulty of achieving anything real or good or important in an impermanent world. But significantly, Odysseus declines Calypso's offer. In losing mortality man will apparently also lose humanness, and as Homer implies, man's life and greatness lie in his humanness. If Odysseus had accepted the offer, he would have become a figure like Popeye, and the poem, rather than confronting the human issues that are the archetypal themes of literature, would have become a ritual piece of sorts, one offering words of advice and comfort to men, not a work about man for man. It would have given a solution that was really no solution at all, only a substitute for confrontation.

It is to the point to note that when Odysseus descends to the Underworld, he asks the shade of the great Achilles how it feels to be Prince of Death. Achilles replies, in effect, that it is better to be a slave and alive than a king and dead, continuing the issue that was at the heart of his brooding in the *Iliad*. It is necessary to be alive, not dead; it is also necessary to be humanly alive, not immortal. Life has, as the *Odyssey* presents it, an existential reality of its own, a reality that all great literature seems to realize. And this literature points further to the necessity of confronting life. In Popeye one escapes from the problems of life. In *The Rime of the Ancient Mariner* one is ostensibly offered platitudes and aphorisms as a basis for life. In the *Odyssey* one is presented with the reality of life.

It is thus possible to examine these three works not only in terms of their superficial forms or techniques, their plots, characters, and settings; it is also necessary to relate and separate them according to how they create meaning—that is, how they use signification—and finally according to how the archetypal themes of literature in general are revealed in them. By so

relating and so separating them, it is possible both to understand them and to judge them. Popeye is entertaining and relax-
ing; *The Rime of the Ancient Mariner* is instructive; but the
Odyssey, like *Moby Dick,* goes far beyond being entertaining
or even instructive. Popular morality has only a superficial
existence in it. The reader is brought into the work and
transported by means of the symbolism far beyond the particular and local significances presented on the narrative level.
It is this involvement in reality and transcending it that is possible in great works of literature.

CHAPTER 4

The Idea of Poetry

One of the very real difficulties in the study of literature is the inadequate critical terminology we must use. As Northrop Frye has pointed out, we lack terms to describe certain genres. Our main term for all long prose fiction, for instance, is *novel;* but many works of prose fiction, like *Gulliver's Travels,* are hardly novels. Certain terms, moreover, have very imprecise meanings. When these terms—*fiction* is one of them—appear in traditional dichotomies, the confusion is increased. A dichotomy like "fact versus fiction" gets in the way of our understanding the terms making up the phrase; repeated hearing of the dichotomy requires a distinct effort if we want to view either of the elements except in terms of its mate. That is, we tend to think of fiction in terms of fact or, more precisely, in terms of nonfact. The statement "That which is not a fact is a fiction" comes oddly to sound like "That which is not true is false." Most of us would probably hesitate to accept the conclusions of the latter statement and say that all fiction is a lie and the writers of fiction are liars. But perhaps without giving conscious thought to the matter, we do tend to view fiction as something less than fact. Fact is real, fiction is made up—a "figment of the imagination." Most of us do not even know what a "figment" is, but we all know that figments of the imagination are to be scorned; they are not "real."

Writers throughout history have justified their imaginative productions by asserting that they are accounts of real or historical events and people. In the twelfth century Geoffrey of Monmouth included a lengthy account of King Arthur and his adventures in a chronicle of the kings of Britain, a chronicle, he said, that he was only copying. He was not, so Geoffrey insisted, making up the stories he penned; they existed as history and in old trusted books to boot. Such claims were typical in the Middle Ages, but other ages produced even more involved statements of historicity or veracity. Jonathan Swift in the eighteenth century constructed a circumstantial frame for *Gulliver's Travels* designed to make his audience believe in the actuality of Lemuel Gulliver and in the fact of his travels to fantastic places. Likewise Daniel Defoe, in what is often regarded as the first English novel, took pains to make his audience believe that Robinson Crusoe existed and that Defoe was presenting an actual biographical account.

Both the writer and the fiction seem always to have been looked down upon. In ancient Greece, Plato would have excluded writers from his ideal republic. In the Middle Ages, St. Thomas Aquinas viewed reading fiction as unprofitable activity that could only delude man and make him indulge in idleness. In more modern times, the Puritans likewise objected to fiction; and many youths today are berated by practical parents for "just reading a novel" instead of doing something "useful."

Perhaps the best way to understand this alleged *bête noire,* fiction, is to view it in terms of how it handles reality. Whereas fact is limited to what is or what has happened and is now over, fiction is concerned with what is possible. Fiction may include fact, but fact, by definition, must exclude the complications, innuendoes, ramifications, and possibilities of what is being said. When the defense attorney at a trial wants to limit the prosecutor's questions, he will insist that the prosecutor "stick to the facts." Nothing circumstantial, conjectural, or even predictable is allowed. The facts must be shaved clean and seen as clearly as possible with all ambiguities removed.

It is fiction that investigates the implications that fact must ignore. Whether the story we are reading actually occurred is beside the point; what is important is that it could or might have happened. Fictional art—indeed, art in general—deals with the possible. To say that it should deal with fact is like insisting that the painter create pictures which look like photographs. Sometimes the reproduction of what is before the eyes is not the most desirable thing; to see the unfamiliar in the familiar and, of course, vice versa, is often more important. It is the artist, shaping the confusion of experience, who gives the world a new insight into the nature of reality.

Just as the fact-fiction dichotomy is inadequate and misleading, so is another: "prose versus poetry." Again the problem is a confusion of terms. An implication of this phrase is that everything we term poetry is not prose. But poetry, at least as we have been speaking of it so far, is a qualitative term, something describing the artistic quality of a given work. We have said that poetry is the most intense connotative language, and to develop a working definition we may now add that poetry comes about when the literary artist says something significant in the best of all possible ways—that is, in the most concise and connotative way. But this definition hardly describes the prose-poetry dichotomy, because prose can be highly connotative and much prose, in fact, contains fine poetry, in the sense of the present definition. Melville, Joseph Conrad, and William Faulkner are only three of many writers who have written novels containing sections that may justifiably be termed poetry; and many critics feel that the best English poet of the twentieth century may well be James Joyce, cited especially for his "novels," *Ulysses* and *Finnegan's Wake*.

In the prose-poetry dichotomy the terms *poetry* and *prose* really stand for forms, and what is termed *poetry* may be more precisely called *verse*. That is, prose is a form of writing that has as its basic structural units the sentence and the paragraph, and verse is a form that uses the line rather than the sentence, and the stanza rather than the paragraph. The distinction between the two forms is not one of content—both prose and verse may have the same matter—or of genre or style—prose may be lyrical, verse may be narrative. Rather, to emphasize the point, the distinction is entirely of form; and the old half-humorous definition of verse as that which has an even left-hand margin and an uneven right-hand one is more exact than might at first be realized.

While making distinctions between prose and verse, we must also realize that either one can be poetry—the qualitative term. Earlier in a discussion of connotative language we looked at two nursery rhymes, "Mary had a little lamb" and "Hey, diddle, diddle, the cat and the fiddle," both of which are in verse. Through its use of connotative language, the second approaches being poetic. In contrast, the earlier prose quotation from Stephen Crane's "Open Boat" is more poetic than the prosaic "Mary had a little lamb."

The trouble in terminology may have come about because traditionally verse was the language of connotative writing (or poetry). Unlike the everyday language of ordinary human affairs, it did not try to be colloquial, familiar, or "natural." It was prophetic and oracular, and since it was oral, it was structured by patterns of rhythm and sound that continued, even reinforced, the verbal ambiguity, and that acted as memory aids for the listener. We all know that verse is easier to remember than prose, and the human animal, in his childhood at least, instinctively responds to verse much more than to prose. We have all heard the chants of children accompanying their play, the jump-rope songs of girls, for instance. But when the child gets older, he becomes more a part of the world of business, the adult world of facts; and prose is more serviceable to him than verse, which gradually comes to seem strange and artificial. Similarly, the earliest literature coming down to us from antiquity, the Middle Ages, or primitive cultures is invariably verse rather than prose, which is ordinarily a latecomer as a literary language. We would do well to remember that in English, for example, prose does not become the ordinary language of fiction until the eighteenth century; but the earliest fiction in verse dates from about the eighth century—a difference of a thousand years.

The inspired language written in verse was thus traditionally synonymous with poetry; but after written (as opposed to oral) compositions became the norm, prose increasingly became a legitimate vehicle for connotative writing. Unfortunately, however, the term *poetry* continued to mean "compositions in verse"; and works that showed no artistry and no connotation but happened to be in verse were grouped under this term. I have no intention of trying to change the popular terminology, and I will continue to call verse compositions *poems*. But I will reserve the term *poetry* for those highly connotative compositions that show the fulfillment of literary art. As a final clarification, *poems* are to be seen as using a form different from *prose* pieces—though it must be recognized that the two forms are becoming increasingly blended and the distinctions increasingly blurred—and *poetry* is a qualitative term whose opposite is *nonpoetry*.

Problems still exist, however, because some works—including some compositions in verse—are both poetic and nonpoetic. Intense, inspired language is hardly the norm and is not easy for even a good writer to sustain. In any long work it is especially difficult for a writer to keep from becoming prosaic. I tend to agree with Edgar Allan Poe that poetry must of necessity be short, because it is too demanding on both author and audience to be so involved continuously. Reading a sonnet by Shakespeare, for example, is an arduous—though, if well done, rewarding—act; it takes all one's concentration and all one's ability at comprehending connotative language. Reading sonnets—there are 154 by Shakespeare—is completely different from reading a novel. The best sonnets are so intense that to try to read more than a handful at one sitting will produce bewilderment; the mind will wander as a defense against the continuous barrage of intense language. As Poe said, a work like John Milton's *Paradise Lost,* an epic of over 10,000 lines, must almost of necessity be quantitatively more unpoetic than poetic. The work contains flashes of great poetry, but much of it can only be termed nonpoetry. It is significant that of the twelve books of the poem the first two show the most intense and connotative language. After these books Milton seems to have wearied with the effort; besides, the scope and nature of the narrative are such that many passages can hardly be poetic.

The writer of the long poem is like the novelist or any writer of long prose fiction: he neither has to nor can he be concerned with each term in his work. There are so many other necessities —such as the development of the plot and characters making up the work's narrative level—that each particular phrase or term must often be neglected if the work is to be finished. It would seem that the larger the canvas, the less time the artist has to worry about each brushstroke; and the smaller the canvas, the more care he can and must take. Consequently, the most connotative and intense of literary works—the one most difficult to read and comprehend—is usually the short lyric poem. The writer of the lyric can spend days, even weeks or months, working over a particular word, producing a work that needs, indeed demands, close critical analysis.

A poem that has become a classic example of concise connotative language is Ezra Pound's "In a Station of the Metro." I quote the entire poem:

> The apparition of these faces in the crowd:
> Petals on a wet, black bough.[1]

According to the author's account of its creation, the poem was originally based on an experience of seeing several beautiful faces one day in the Paris subway. Pound tried all that day to describe the experience, but as he said, "I could not find any

[1] Ezra Pound, *Personae,* "In a Station of the Metro." Copyright © 1926, 1954 by Ezra Pound. Reprinted by permission of the publisher, New Directions Publishing Corporation.

words that seemed to me worthy, or as lovely as that sudden emotion." He first wrote a thirty-line poem but destroyed it because it was a work "of second intensity." Six months later he penned a poem of half that length, and a year later he wrote the above two lines. During this year the original expression was apparently so fashioned and so polished that everything unnecessary was removed. Aside from the prepositions and articles, all the terms function connotatively and suggest much more than one might realize at first reading. Even the title acts as a necessary part of the poem, for it locates and limits the action. Without it we would not understand the basis in reality for the two lines that follow, but with it we understand the particular subject being described.

In this poem we view a station in the Paris subway, with a train coming out of the darkness. Inside are the passengers; perhaps their faces are at the windows, or perhaps they are seen as they enter and leave the train. In any case, we are conscious of only their faces—lighted ovals in contrast to the train, which is dark and, as the next line suggests, wet. We know that the faces are to suggest to us the people that are there; through the rhetorical device of synecdoche, the part is made to stand for the whole. But Pound also has particular reasons for making us conscious of the faces. Described as an *apparition,* they appear as something unreal; they are like floating lights in the hollowness of the station, contrasting with the pervading darkness. Perhaps we cannot see the rest of them because their bodies are covered with clothing, dark clothing apparently; but such a statement is merely a "logical" explanation of the scene before our eyes. The poet's concern is not to state the realistic but to create a certain consciousness or awareness in his readers. He has presented us with human beings, but in emphasizing the faces—more precisely, in speaking of "The apparition of these faces"—he has changed the human into something else and has brought into his poem something eerie. The familiar has become the unfamiliar, and the spectral, the mysterious, now at hand, is influencing our further view of the scene.

But *faces* not only relates to *apparition;* the term must also be seen in terms of *crowd*—a word whose function may best be understood by substituting some similar word for it. Should *crowd* be changed to, say, *group,* the meaning of the phrase would be distinctly altered. There would then be suggested a sense of relationship among the individual faces. The term *group* would imply a homogeneity not found in *crowd:* a group serves to unify its particular members; a crowd allows for, even insists on, the anonymity of those who make it up (we cannot even speak of the *members* of a crowd). Another possible substitution for *crowd* is *mob;* but as with *group,* the implication is that its individual parts are united with a common purpose is a band—one can be a member of a mob. The term *crowd,* however, implies an aloneness, even a loneliness, which goes along with the implications of *apparition* and of the seemingly detached faces.

One final word in this line should receive comment—*these.* We have *the* apparition and *the* crowd, but between them are *these* faces. What is being seen is particularized; we are being made aware of the faces before us not as any kind of collective entity but as individuals. Conversely, it would be against the meaning of the line to change *the* crowd to *this* crowd. The poet is not speaking of a particular collective entity, but he does want us to think of the faces as individual. Furthermore, the term *these* puts the faces immediately in front of us. Had Pound said *those* faces, for instance, our attention would have been directed to something apart from us; but with *these* he is referring to what is around us—perhaps our faces are even in the crowd. Both the image and the meaning of the line are made more immediate because of the pronoun. The distinct impression of this first line is one of alienation, loneliness, a wandering without purpose. The words and the phrases act to give us not just a mental image but also a view of man, who appears here as detached and homeless—a pathetic spectre.

The second line, literally in apposition with the first, may also be seen as a comment on it and a further statement about the human condition. *Petals* would seem to be a development of *faces* in the first line, both being the only plural nouns in the poem and both giving the same impression—something light-colored, detached, and, as Pound would have us see them, fragile. The petals that are called to our attention are not the entire blossoms; they are detached from their stems as the faces seem to be from their bodies. Furthermore, the petals are on a "wet, black bough," each word is stressed and the monosyllables are harsh. The petals are hardly growing on this bough. Had the poet said *stem* instead of *bough,* the impression would have been entirely different. As it stands, the image shows the petals as uprooted; they seem to be stuck to the "wet, black bough." Apparently brought there by a rain storm, they will stick until the bough dries, and then they will fall away from this temporary resting place.

These fragile petals are not only like the ghostly faces of the first line; they also suggest the existence of the people in the crowd. Even though the bough may be visually associated with the train—the shapes may be seen as possibly similar—the real association is with the crowd. Both bough and crowd are alive —we can see how different the effect of the second line would have been had Pound written "Petals on a wet, black *log"*—but ironically neither bough nor crowd is really supporting life. The helpless petals are on the bough purely by chance and may be lifted off with the next breeze. They will be tossed by the wind until they fall to the ground. So, it would seem, with human beings, with the faces that appear in the crowd for only a moment. They drift apart and away as petals in the wind.

The analogy between the situation in nature and that of man follows upon and continues the relationships of the first line. "These faces" appeared there at the center of our attention. They were seen as unreal and in an uncaring environment, a fact emphasized in the second line where the uncaring environment is shown to be that of life in general; the petals in this line are, as it were, in the same predicament as man. Moreover, man, who is not in control of his existence, is ironically a helpless petal. The setting brought out in the title of the poem shows man between start and finish; the station of the metro is merely a point of pause. Also the setting is without glamour; had Pound used, say, an airport or a ship instead of a subway, the impression would have been entirely different.

As the two lines stand, they tend to be ironic, bitter, and full of pathos, although their author certainly exhibits a sympathy toward his subject. They reveal an aspect—perhaps the dominant one—of the human situation and create our response to it. Everything in the lines is functional—even, as will be seen later, the sound patterns and the rhythms. But we must be capable of receiving the awareness the lines offer us. Once our ear is attuned to the subtle and the sublime, we find our awarenesses, even our understandings, developing. When we respond, we do so, as it were, with the author. It is not that Pound has a "message" here for us. He has made us focus our attention on a bit of reality we may not have seen before in his way; he has changed our focal point and had us see the familiar from a new angle and in a new way. Our perception is sharpened; and with the sharpening, the familiar and the commonplace become transformed. This brief poem is more than a piece of decorative imagery, more than a pretty picture or a collection of interesting sounds and rhythms. It has a meaning, but one that cannot be said in any way other than as Pound says it. We can paraphrase these lines and show in page after page how their terms function, but if asked what the poem is saying, we can answer only by reading it aloud. The poem is its own statement of meaning, and while referring to familiar reality, it has a reality all its own that cannot be paraphrased or restated, much as we try. In Archibald Mac-Leish's famous statement, "A poem should not mean but be." Pound's "In a Station of the Metro" has an existence that

makes it and what it is saying continually relevant and continually new.

A classic illustration of the opposite of the conciseness and
connotation found in this poem may be seen in Henry Wads-
worth Longfellow's "A Psalm of Life." Too long to be quoted
here in its entirety (and not worth the space), the poem is a
pastiche of the familiar, the commonplace, and the hackneyed.
A few stanzas will illustrate its methods and its inadequacies:

> Tell me not, in mournful numbers,
>   Life is but an empty dream!—
> For the soul is dead that slumbers,
>   And things are not what they seem.
>
> Life is real! Life is earnest!
>   And the grave is not its goal;
> Dust thou art, to dust returnest,
>   Was not spoken of the soul.
>
> .   .   .   .
>
> In the world's broad field of battle,
>   In the bivouac of Life,
> Be not like dumb, driven cattle!
>   Be a hero in the strife!
>
> Trust no Future, how'er pleasant!
>   Let the dead Past bury its dead!
> Act,—act in the living Present!
>   Heart within, and God o'erhead!

And on it goes, giving good advice in the form of moral
clichés. The images lack completely the freshness found in
those in "In a Station of the Metro"; they exist as a series of
canned platitudes. Rather than stimulate our awareness and
feeling, Longfellow grabs and drags in everything that would
seem to have in our society a built-in emotional and moral
value. In "A Psalm of Life" popular morality is presented as a
substitute for poetry.

But the response to this poem and similar ones by those who do not understand poetry seems to be "If the advice is good, the statement of it must also be good," or even something like "A poem about God cannot be bad but must of necessity be better than a poem about garbage." The error of such statements should be obvious. The homilist and the poet are two different beings: the first has preaching and teaching as his means and end; the second probes beneath the surface and reveals what is found there. The first is a purveyor of traditional morality; the second often creates a morality of his own. Poetry, like all art, cannot be subject to the moral or ethical criteria of daily life. When we say that a poem is good or bad, we are talking about its artistry, not making a value judgment about the merits of its themes; similarly, when we say a poem is right or wrong, we are speaking of its total impact, the way it succeeds in doing what it has set out to do. As Henry James wrote, we must allow writers their *données,* their assumptions or givens, then see and judge what they do with these. Consequently, no subject can have a built-in superiority to any other subject, and the poem about garbage can be more "moral" (and better written) than the poem about God. We may agree with Longfellow's sentiments and even with his idea of writing a psalm of life; but at the same time we can wish he had done a better job. His poem is a bad poem—it is nonpoetry—for many reasons. Its singsong rhythm clashes with the philosophical seriousness of its words; its parts do not all contribute to a total effort; its theme is overstated; and its language is more denotative than connotative and when it is connotative it is hackneyed. The poem does not tell us anything we did not know. Rather than make us aware, it lulls us with the trite and true, the old favorites that are sure to make it acceptable.

Such criticism is not meant to suggest that a poem cannot be moral or religious—the Bible itself is, of course, often very poetical—and it may even be argued that poetry is of necessity religious. But this is to use *religious* as a term implying a concern for or an awareness of the mystery, even the holiness, of life. The following piece by the contemporary writer William Packard is religious in this sense:

> forever is a wide sky & heaven is
> no heaviness inside our heads & no
> great hatred in our hearts, it is
> the quiet eye, it is the secret peace
> at the still center of the will,
> it is what no one can know, & yet
> whoever sees the mystery & bliss
> of this shall surely come into
> the presence of serenity

The concerns here are those we associate with religion; the tone is prophetic, the words deal with the metaphysical—and the piece is very effective. But it is effective not *because* of its subject matter per se. Rather, the ideas of *forever* and *heaven* are being redefined; and at the end of this long drawn-out sentence, which sounds remarkably like a benediction, we have experienced a new awareness of these ideas. Similarly, the success of the piece is due not to the presence of the prophetic and the metaphysical, but to the way these are used. Everything —words, sounds, tones, and rhythms—contributes to the poem's effect—and to its effectiveness; and when we reach the end of the thought, the benediction is completed and perfected, and we actually "come into the presence of serenity." The poet has thus created what his words are saying. Old ideas become alive and meaningful here in a way they may not have been for many of us. Also, the poem is not something existing in a never-never land apart from man and his immediate situation. Its relevance to our life should be apparent on even the most casual reading, and, moreover, we are brought into the piece as Packard refers to "our heads" and "our hearts" and to what we can know and see. We join the author in the new insights and in the real and continuous experience of the poem.

That connotative writing may appear simple and unadorned

and even be in a rhythm like that of "A Psalm of Life" can be seen in several old English and Scottish ballads. A well-known example is "Sir Patrick Spens," which in its earliest extant version goes as follows:

1   The king sits in Dumferling toune,
      Drinking the blude-reid wine:
   'O whar will I get guid sailor,
      To sail this schip of mine?'

2   Up and spak an eldern knicht,
      Sat at the kings richt kne:
   'Sir Patrick Spens is the best sailor
      That sails upon the se.'

3   The king has written a braid letter,
      And signd it wi his hand,
   And sent it to Sir Patrick Spens,
      Was walking on the sand.

4   The first line that Sir Patrick red,
      A loud lauch lauched he;
   The next line that Sir Patrick red,
      The teir blinded his ee.

5   'O wha is this has don this deid,
      This ill deid don to me,
   To send me out this time o' the yeir,
      To sail upon the se!

6   'Mak haste, mak haste, my mirry men all,
      Our guid schip sails the morne.'
   'O say na sae, my master deir,
      For I feir a deadlie storme.

7   'Late late yestreen I saw the new moone,
      Wi the auld moone in hir arme,
   And I feir, I feir, my deir master,
      That we will cum to harme.'

8   O our Scots nobles were richt laith
     To weet their cork-heild schoone;
     Bot lang owre a' the play wer playd,
     Thair hats they swam aboone.

9   O lang, lang may their ladies sit,
     Wi thair fans into their hand,
     Or eir they se Sir Patrick Spens
     Cum sailing to the land.

10 O lang, lang may their ladies stand,
     Wi thair gold kems in their hair,
     Waiting for thair ain deir lords,
     For they'll se thame na mair.

11 Haf owre, haf owre to Aberdour,
     It's fiftie fadom deip,
     And thair lies guid Sir Patrick Spens,
     Wi the Scots lords at his feit.

The important thing about this ballad is not whether the story
it is telling is true—that is, whether the poem is a record of
historical fact. Rather, we should focus on the breadth of the
story, the economy of language, the emotional power, and the
drama found in these eleven stanzas. On the surface this ballad
may seem very different from "In a Station of the Metro," but
the only significant differences are, first, that it uses a narrative
rather than a picture to convey its theme and, second, that it
was designed to be heard rather than read from a book. Its
language is consequently that of speech rather than writing.
Even if we should think of Longfellow's "A Psalm of Life" as
a song, this ballad is also different from that piece. Here there
are no directions for the audience; there is only a compelling
story that contains its own meaning. Here also, as opposed to
the Longfellow piece, the simple ballad rhythm blends with the
language and the subject.

Still the language, albeit homely and colloquial, is often
connotative. For instance, in the second line the wine the king

is drinking is termed *blude-reid,* bloodred. The color seems unimportant in itself; it presents implications not about the wine but rather about the king and the action to follow. Had the wine been described as, say, *rosy-reid,* the tone and point would have been altered. As it stands, *blude-reid* acts as a forecast of things to come—specifically, the death of Sir Patrick and his men—and associates the king who is drinking it with the deaths. But even at first reading, even before we know what follows, *blude-reid* serves as an ominous suggestion of imminent disaster.

At other times the language is made connotative through structural parallels and contrasts. For instance, again at the beginning of the poem, the king is shown *sitting* in the city, a description that may seem innocuous until we get to the end of the third stanza and see Sir Patrick "walking on the sand." While the king sits safely in his palace enjoying the material comfort of his wine, Sir Patrick and his men must experience all sorts of dangers on the open seas, far from the safety of the city. It is also to be noted that Sir Patrick's name is given to the king by an "eldern knicht" who "Sat at the kings richt kne." This scene of king with lords at his feet is ironically repeated at the end of the poem where we see "guid Sir Patrick Spence / Wi the Scots lords at his feit." Even though dead, the heroes are shown as noble and in a regal position corresponding to that seen in the king's court. And, indeed, Sir Patrick himself is contrasted with the king who sent him out to his death. Sir Patrick is the better man by far, implies the poet; and his court "fiftie fadom deip" is implicitly better than the king's. The wine the king drinks gives way to the water Sir Patrick and his men consumed as they drowned. This implicit comparison is far from being humorous, and Sir Patrick is no whit the less regal.

A third way in which connotative language is created in this poem is through repetition. An example of this is found in the first two lines of stanza five: " 'O wha is this has don this deid, / This ill deid don to me.' " These words, Sir Patrick's first in the poem and his response to the king's letter, contain more than a gratuitous repetition. The first line shows Sir Patrick's amazement at what is being asked of him and his feeling that he has been betrayed by some false counselor to the king. The second line seems to show the same thing, but the mere fact of the repetition itself adds to our awareness of how impossible are the king's orders. We are made aware of the danger in what Sir Patrick must do, and the incremental repetition—the development of *deid* to *ill deid*—drives home the point.

A similar kind of incremental repetition that makes the language of the poem connotative is found in stanza four. Here there is a distinct progression of thought and response. As we read the first two lines, we do not know why Sir Patrick is laughing; but after we read the last two lines, we understand the absurdity of the king's command, the bitterness of Sir Patrick's response, and the danger of the voyage. Still a further instance of incremental repetition—again with a result of irony —is found in stanzas nine and ten. The ladies with their fans and combs, like the king earlier, are ironically contrasted with the heroes who have died. But it is the repetition of the "O lang, lang . . ." lines and the progression from *sit* to *stand* that we have seen elsewhere in the poem that make us feel the irony.

Also found in stanzas nine and ten is a fourth method of creating connotation—the method of indirect understatement. The poet never says that the Scots lords are dead; his most direct statement of what happens to them is in the final stanza, the eleventh one. But in nine and ten he talks about fine ladies with fans and combs. These are what remain, and they will, says the poet bitterly, remain waiting "lang, lang." The poet seems to have ambivalent feelings about these ladies. They are the wives and loves of the dead Scots lords, and in this connection they are to be pitied. But they are also associated with the court—as they sit with their fans and stand with their combs— and for this association they are to be scorned. With dramatic irony the poet makes us aware of how they fail to comprehend what has happened. We understand though and feel the bitter death, whereas the fine ladies are apparently only sitting preening themselves. If they knew, they would—or should—be tearing their hair.

The best illustration of how an indirect—especially an ambiguous—statement can be connotative is found in stanza eight. Literally, the four lines say, "Oh, our Scots nobles really hated to wet their cork-heeled shoes; but long before all the play was finished, their hats swam above them (or perhaps their shoes swam above their hats)." The first two lines sound as though the Scots nobles are fops who are afraid of getting their feet wet, but—and here is the bitter humor again—they ironically end up with the water reaching to and over their hats. The syntactic confusion of the last two lines seems very much to the point because the poet is indirectly stating the result of the ill-fated voyage.

Throughout this stanza and the next three the poet proceeds from being most indirect to being least indirect, and it is almost with incredulity that we comprehend what has happened. The final four stanzas make us increasingly aware of the fact of the death, and the poet's—and our—anger and bitterness increase. The four stanzas preceding these forecast the death as they make us aware of the time of year—apparently winter and no time for sailing; of an imminent "deadlie storme"; of cosmic suggestions of danger—"the new moone, / Wi the auld moone in hir arme"; and of *feir*—repeated several times. But when we understand fully that Sir Patrick and his men have died, we are still shocked. The poet has created a suspense that is developed from the first stanza of the poem, and our awareness of the tragedy, far from relieving this suspense, justifies it.

The lines of the poem move quickly and carry the story to its conclusion. We are carried before we know it from the city to the shore where we see Sir Patrick reading his letter; we listen to his response and see him hurrying to carry out the king's orders; we witness his premonition of disaster, reinforced by the words of one of his sailors; and then we have the death. There has been no wasted motion, no excess of any sort. The economy of handling makes us aware of how much could be said and is actually being implied here. But this dramatic, tightly constructed narrative is not the poet's main concern. If it were, he surely would have described in detail the shipwreck and death of Sir Patrick and the Scots lords. As the poem stands, however, such a depiction would be apart from, and would even negate, his purpose. It is not the fact or manner of the death but the irony of it that the poet wants to bring out.

He seems, moreover, to be using the story of Sir Patrick Spens as a vehicle for political or social protest. Even if Sir Patrick was not intentionally murdered—by the false counselor who suggested his name—his life was at least squandered, and needlessly so. The king should have known better than to command Sir Patrick to sail, but no matter how foolish the command, Sir Patrick obeyed his king just as Sir Patrick's own men loyally obeyed him. We are made aware at the same time of something grand and heroic: although Sir Patrick is destroyed, he is also made noble. With the irony and the waste comes a sense of greatness.

CHAPTER 5

Methods of the Poem

As was said earlier, in understanding how a poem works it is ultimately unimportant whether its narrative level is an account of an actual situation or a description of an existing scene. When we ask about the historicity of the subject, we are going from the work back to the world that gave it its materials; the questions may be interesting, but we must recognize that they take us far from the poem. Doubtless there was in "Sir Patrick Spens," for example, a particular story—actual or not—that represented the ultimate source of what appears in the poem as quoted here; and doubtless there was a particular intention on the part of the author that was the efficient cause of his creating this poem. But all the particulars that have gone into the work have become transformed so that the work has a meaning and gives an impression all its own. The points of references are no longer in, say, Scotland of the fifteenth century; the poem is effective and meaningful to us not because of the historical situation—if there was one. Rather, it has transcended the historical fact and approached a truth that is ever present. It is this truth that, as Garcia Lorca says, is found in poetry.

A perceptive and effective depiction of how poetry is created is found in a poem by the contemporary writer John Balaban:

Nicely like a pearl is a poem;
begun with an accidental speck of sand
from the ocean of the actual.

A grain, a grit,
which, once admitted,
slowly
irritates the mantle of thought,
coating itself
in the perfecting lacquers of the mind.

The particular incident or interest that starts the poem is the "accidental speck of sand." It could have been any speck—the "ocean of the actual" is indeed large—but it happened, willy-nilly, to be a particular one. What the poet then creates from this particular thing no more resembles it than a pearl resembles the speck of sand that was at the basis of its existence. Nor is the transformation of gritty reality into poetry a change from the more real to the less real: a pearl is as "real" as a grain of sand, the difference is that the pearl is beautiful, compelling, and worth something to us.

This quotation reveals the miracle of the process of poetry, a miracle like that of the transformation of the grain of sand into a pearl or the metamorphosis of a caterpillar into a butterfly. No matter how well we understand or think we understand the process, it is always mysterious, awesome, even unbelievable. The process of poetry is, moreover, not complete even when the grain, working in the mind of the poet, has been transformed into the poem. The process continues as the poem is read, and every reading is, in a sense, a re-creation of it and of the miracle of its existence. Poetry is also a living thing, and as such it must of necessity irritate. The birth of a poem is not often easy, because irritating the mantle of the poet's thought, it forces itself to be created. And once born, it must continue to irritate sensitive readers and listeners of all times and places. Poetry may be something beautiful, something that orders chaos, but at the same time it must disturb those who approach it and compel them to reevaluate and reinterpret.

The work that soothes and placates is, as we have seen, not poetry. True poetry is most often asymmetrical and dissonant, not symmetrical and harmonious. Let us look for a moment at the following translation of a Japanese *haiku* by Taniguchi Buson, called by its translator, Harold G. Henderson, "The Sudden Chillness":

> The piercing chill I feel:
> My dead wife's comb, in our bedroom,
> Under my heel . . .[1]

We would be hard put to say what the "meaning" of this poem is, but the shock, the realization, we feel contains and expresses in itself the meaning. These three lines have created an awareness, albeit a discomforting one; and we might well ask why. Here is a prose statement of the three lines: "While in the bedroom I felt my dead wife's comb under my heel; I was conscious of a piercing chill." This statement contains the idea of the poem, but all the shock and relevance are gone. But, significantly, they are not gone even when we return to the poem for subsequent readings. The poetry is not the same as the shock, but the live thing that is poetry will constantly produce this shock, which may be close to what Stephen Spender has called "the shock of recognition."

This brief poem in fact demands that we return to it again and again, not because we do not understand it but because it is so compelling. What might be termed our intuitive awareness of its meaning is what makes us want—indeed need— to read it again. In addition, every bit as important as the words themselves are the rhythms and the sound patterns. Change the order of words and we change the poem and probably its effectiveness—as was demonstrated by the prose rendition. It is thus important for us to realize that poetry is more than a wise or important thought; it is also the saying of this thought.

[1] Harold G. Henderson, *An Introduction to Haiku*. Copyright © 1958 by Harold G. Henderson. Reprinted by permission of Doubleday & Company, Inc.

Poetry may also give a picture. The following sketch by
Walt Whitman, called "Cavalry Crossing a Ford," is in some
ways like Pound's "In a Station of the Metro," though there
the picture was in the form of a metaphor and the scene included us, the audience—that is, if we were not part of it, we
were at least close at hand. In Whitman's poem, however, we
stand with the poet away from the scene, on a hill as it were,
and look down to where he directs our attention:

A line in long array where they wind betwixt green islands,
They take a serpentine course, their arms flash in the sun—hark
        to the musical clank,
Behold the silvery river, in it the splashing horses loitering
        stop to drink,
Behold the brown-faced men, each group, each person a picture,
        the negligent rest on the saddles,
Some emerge on the opposite bank, others are just entering
        the ford—while,
Scarlet and blue and snowy white,
The guidon flags flutter gayly in the wind.

We see the soldiers at the time of the American Civil War as
though they were in an actual painting and, indeed, the poet
speaks of "each person a picture." But Whitman's words produce a verbal painting more dynamic than most paintings.
    The poet first directs our attention to the background where
the brown line of cavalry winds through the green forest—the
colors being as important as the figures of men and horses.
The apparently silver shining of their arms is echoed in the
"silvery river," and the flashing and sounding—"the musical
clank" of the arms—are echoed in the splashing of the horses
and, again, in the silvery shine of the river. We have now been
brought to the foreground of this verbal picture, and as the
horses "loitering stop," so does the picture—for a few moments
at least. In this pause Whitman directs our attention to more
particular details in his scene. The "brown-faced men" are

like part of nature; we look at them in groups and individually as they too stop. Around them is the motion of those entering and leaving that part of the scene that has become frozen before our eyes; in this balanced composition, motion exists on the sides, but quiet and rest are maintained in the center.

But then Whitman almost abruptly turns his and our attention to something that seems to be apart from the scene—the guidon flags in the last two lines—although we should realize that they represent an even closer look at the scene. Our attention is riveted to them and we see them "Scarlet and blue and snowy white" as they "flutter gayly in the wind." Whereas their colors and motion seem to clash with the green and brown to which we have grown accustomed, they relate to and were anticipated by the silver and flashing earlier. Likewise, while their gay fluttering may contrast with the paused men and horses at the center of the picture, it takes us back to the flashing arms at the beginning of the poem. Still, we are surprised as the heaviness suggested by men, horses, forest, and earth is replaced by a feeling of lightness, and as the "serpentine" procession, with weapons of death, becomes full of bright life.

It is this sense of life that represents the poem's final and main comment. The cavalry has been seen in terms of the natural setting through which it proceeded as a snakelike crawling animal. Now a miracle has taken place, and the crawling animal displays a real vitality of its own. It bursts forth in a metamorphosis and flutters gaily and innocently as a butterfly. Whitman's sketch here has thus not only frozen a scene, memorializing it, but has also made us see the scene in a new way. We have had a sense of an extraordinary vision. The poet has used his picture so as to transcend it; and the play of various colors, of silence and sound, of quiet and motion, and of sobriety and gaiety acts to make us aware of interrelationships between the human and the natural, the animate and the inanimate.

Whitman's poem is an example of free verse: it lacks specially patterned rhythms and sounds. It reads, in fact, as though it might be prose until we come to the last two lines, which seem to have a more pronounced and regular rhythm than the five earlier lines. The relative shortness and marked rhythm of "Scarlet and blue and snowy white" emphasize the contrast between the flags and the scene and raise the pitch of the poem above the heavily prosaic. Adding to the lightness of these lines are the several *s, f,* and *l* sounds which also relate the words here to terms appearing earlier; *flutter,* for instance, refers back to *flash.* Still Whitman seems to be thinking throughout this entire piece, not just in the last two lines, in terms of verse lines rather than prose sentences. *While,* for instance, separated on the line preceding the description of the guidons, seems to be intentionally placed by itself; set apart, it creates a pause of expectancy and serves to prepare us for the changes of pace to come. Furthermore, Whitman is using language to create ambiguity, freshness, and vitality; it is hardly accidental, for instance, that the *wind* of the first line should anticipate and parallel the *wind* of the last line—both looking alike though sounding different. The first one, a verb, describes the shape and motion of the line of men; the second one, a noun, represents something above the earth, a state of vitality and exuberance that is our final impression of the scene and that, as has been said, transforms it.

Although there is no space here to give a formal presentation of poetic techniques, it is necessary to insist that readers of poetry understand that words, rhythms, and sounds all act together in patterns to give the work its full meaning. In verse, the rhythm is most often measured, and the sounds, if not patterned as *rhyme,* are at least linked together. Thus, to create, develop, and pattern their meanings, poets use such devices as *assonance,* similarities in vowel sounds; *consonance,* similarities in consonant sounds; and *alliteration,* likenesses in the sounds of the first syllables of words. The sole justification for these patterns is that they aid in producing a statement more effective than is possible using plain sentences of denotative language. These patterns do not, if handled well, make the language flowery or "artificial"; rather, they make it intense. Thus, instead of subordinating his thought to metrical requirements, the skilled poet uses the metrics to develop it, to make it meaningful and effective. In some poems, such as "A Psalm of Life," the meter and rhymes get in the way of the thought; they jar and appear disconcerting. When done well, however, they act as the organizing principle of the poem. Robert Frost's statement that he would just as soon write poems without meter and rhyme as play tennis with the net down is somewhat misleading, because metrics are more than obstacles to Frost, just as the writing of poetry is more than a game. But at the same time, the net is a real and necessary part of tennis, and metrics are such for the writer who needs them—as Whitman does when he describes the flags.

A brief illustration from another poem will show how metrical rhythm works and how an understanding of it is integral to our understanding of poetry:

> Old Eben Flood, climbing alone one night
> Over the hill between the town below
> And the forsaken upland hermitage
> That held as much as he should ever know
> On earth again of home, paused warily.

This is the beginning of a narrative-monologue by Edwin Arlington Robinson called "Mr. Flood's Party." About an old outcast who goes alone into the hills above his town and drinks, remembering the past, the poem shows both sympathy and irony. These five lines, all one lengthy statement, set the stage and mood for what follows.

To see how the metrics work, we should first mark off in each line the important words. Polysyllabic words will be accented according to their ordinary pronunciation. Thus, in the first line, *Eben* will be accented over the first *E, climbing* over the first *i,* and *alone* over the *o.* Furthermore, *Flood,* the title figure's name, will be accented because it is an important word. So will *night,* for the time matters, since the poem would be different if the action described took place in daylight. *Old* is somewhat ambiguous; we may not know at first whether it acts as a term of familiarity or as a real description of age. As the poem develops, however, it becomes increasingly apparent that Eben's age is significant, so the word should probably receive a stress. *One,* however, is a different matter. It obviously does not mean *one* as opposed to *two;* rather, *one* functions here as the preposition *at* would, not as a limiting or describing word. The scene is just one night, not one particular night, and so *one* will probably be unstressed.

Therefore, with *I* standing for stressed syllables and × for unstressed ones,[1] the line may be scanned as follows:

$$\text{\footnotesize} I \quad I \quad × \quad I \quad\quad I \quad I \quad ×I \quad\quad × \quad I$$

Old Eben Flood, climbing alone one night

What must still be done is to mark off the metrical units, the so-called feet, found here. This is done by analyzing the stressed and unstressed syllables according to the patterns that make up ordinary speech. The more common patterns follow:

Iamb—unstress followed by stress, × *I*, as in the words *above* and *below*. Each iambic unit is called a *foot* and is marked off with vertical lines. A line composed of, say, five iambic units would look like this — ×*I* | ×*I* | ×*I* | ×*I* | ×*I* — and would be called an *iambic pentameter* line (Greek *penta* for "five," *meter* for "measure" or "foot"). A line of one foot would be called *monometer;* one of two feet, *dimeter;* three feet, *trimeter;* four feet, *tetrameter;* six feet, *hexameter;* etc.

Troche—stress followed by unstress, *I* ×, the reverse of the iamb, as in the words *góing* and *ónly*. A line made up of four trochees — *I* × | *I* × | *I* × | *I* × | — would be a *trochaic tetrameter* line.

Anapest—in a sense a developed iamb; two unstresses followed by one stress, × × *I*, as in *disappear*. A line of three

---

[1] Other marks may be used; e.g., − for stressed syllables, and ∪ for unstressed ones.

anapests — ××ı | ××ı | ××ı — would be in *anapestic trimeter*.

Dactyl—the reverse of the anapest, in a sense a developed trochee; a stress followed by two unstresses, ı×× , as in *happily*. A line of two dactyls — ı×× | ı×× — would be in *dactylic dimeter*.

Two other patterns found occasionally but not customarily making up an entire line are the *spondee,* two stressed syllables, ı ı ; and the *pyrrhic,* two unstressed syllables, × × .

After noting the stressed and unstressed syllables of the words in a particular line, we should then forget momentarily the usual meter we ascribe to these words, because the metrical pattern may cut through them. To find what kind of feet are present, we should start with the iambs and trochees, the most common patterns in English, and see whether the line may be described and marked off in terms of them; if not, we should then try the anapests and dactyls, with the spondees and pyrrhics held in reserve. Each foot must be a complete one, except for the last foot in the line, which may have a stress with no unstress; but every foot, except, of course, the pyrrhic, needs one stress.

One should also realize that a line may often be made up of several metrical types. For instance, the following one— ı× | ××ı | ×ı | ×ı — begins with a trochee, followed by an anapest and two iambs. For making a general statement about the metrical nature of this line, the majority wins; there are more iambs than any other pattern, so the line would be described as *iambic tetrameter*—*iambic* naming the major pattern, *tetrameter* identifying the total number of feet in the line. If one pattern is not clearly predominant, then the line should be described in terms of its several patterns.

Now back to the first line of "Mr. Flood's Party." Divided into feet, it would look like this:

1   Old E | ben Flood, | climbing | alone | one night

The line contains five feet, the first spondaic, the second iambic, the third trochaic, the fourth and fifth iambic again. The line is thus generally in iambic pentameter. The next four lines of this passage may be scanned as follows:

```
      /    x    x   /    x   /     x    /     x   /
2   Over | the hill | between | the town | below
      x    x    x /   x    /    x    /     x  x
3   And the | forsa | ken up | land her | mitage
      x   /     x   /    x   /    x    /   x    /
4   That held | as much | as he | should e | ver know
      x   /    x   /   x    /     /      /    xx
5   On earth | again | of home, | paused wa | rily.
```

Articles, conjunctions, auxiliary verbs, and monosyllabic prepositions are ordinarily without stress; the more important words —nouns, descriptive adjectives and adverbs, and verbs of action—are ordinarily with stress. But the point of metrical analysis is to do more than cover the poem with slashes and x's. It is to see how the rhythm works in terms of the meaning of the poem. To begin understanding this, we should notice the exceptions to the dominant rhythm of any line.

The basic metrical pattern in lines 2 through 5 is still the iambic pentameter found in line 1. Line 2, however, begins with a trochee, line 3 with a pyrrhic (it also seems to end with one, though the *-age* in *hermitage* may be partially stressed by some speakers). Line 4 is regularly iambic, as is line 5 until the next-to-last foot, where there appears a spondee, followed by another pyrrhic. These exceptions may be seen as representing instances where Robinson has chosen to vary his basic iambic rhythm. We should understand why, or, more precisely, we should see how these exceptions function.

The poem began in its first line with the name of the main character, followed by the present participle *climbing* that starts a phrase which then goes on without delay or punctuation until it reaches the comma and the word *paused* in the fifth line. But *climbing* itself functions in two ways. First, as a present participle, it makes the action appear to be happening at the time of reading—a characteristic of *-ing* parts of the verb— producing in the reader a sense of immediacy. Second, *climbing* is a trochee, which contrasts with and plays against the dominant iambic pattern. With this word in its different rhythm, we begin climbing, as it were, and do not stop until Eben does. When, in fact, we read these five lines, we find we are called upon to speak them in one breath—or at least they move in a single breath from the comma after *Flood* to the one before *paused.* And when we reach this comma and the word *paused,* we are ready to stop. The connectives *over* and *between* in line 2 introduce prepositional phrases that push the thought and the climb along; similarly, *and* in line 3 makes it continue, *that* in 4 introduces a subordinate clause which carries the thought still further, and the prepositions *on* and *of* in line 5 function as did the earlier *over* and *between.* It is also significant that each line after the first begins with a connective that keeps us from pausing.

But *over,* a trochee like *climbing,* plays likewise against the basic iambic rhythm and continues the sense of effort, as do the pyrrhics at the beginning and end of 3, which make us go on without even the slight pause of a stress. The pace in fact quickens until we reach the comma and the word *paused* in line 5. The phrase "paused warily," with its spondee and subsequent dropping-off pyrrhic, contrasts with the basic rhythm. But the heavy syllables of the spondee really stop the action, so that it is only proper for a dropping-off and a full stop—signaled by a period here—to follow. We might even discover in reading the passage that we have pronounced *warily* as though it were *wearily,* a feeling suggested by the movement of the lines and suggested by the form of *warily.* The main thought of these lines has now reached its climax and conclusion; the next line of the poem will begin a new thought, but one using the atmosphere and implications created in this opening passage.

The lines are also held together by certain patterns of sound. A series of long vowels, especially [o] and [i], add to the heaviness and weariness suggested by the rhythm and words—for instance, old, alone, over, below, know, home; and Eben, between, and he. The other dominant long vowel sound, [aI], as in climbing, and night, may act to continue the heaviness;

but it seems more to rise from it as the word *climbing,* with its trochaic rhythm, contrasts with the main rhythm. The shorter [ʌ] sounds also permeate the passage in Fl*o*od, *o*ne, *u*pland, and m*u*ch, as do the [ər] sound of h*er*mitage, *ear*th, ev*er*, and ov*er*.

The dominant consonant sounds in the passage are the nasals [m] and [n]—as in Ebe*n,* cli*m*bing, alo*ne,* o*ne,* *n*ight, betwee*n,* tow*n,* forsake*n,* etc. The nasal appears in each of the five lines. The [h] sound is also found in quantity here—*h*ill, *h*ermitage, *h*eld, *h*e, *h*ome—perhaps having an echoic function of giving a sense of breathlessness, in imitation, in a sense, of Eben's panting from the climb and of our being short of breath from saying the passage without stopping. It is interesting, and significant, that the words "paused warily" do not contain any of the dominant sound elements of the passage. These words, set apart after the comma and by their different rhythms, do not fit into the climb; they are, as it were, its end and opposite.

To summarize: these five lines of "Mr. Flood's Party" suggest, first, loneliness and sadness, and second, a sense of movement, a journey in darkness away from the light, the town, and the companionship ordinarily found there. Such words as *old, alone, forsaken,* and *hermitage* and the combinations of words and phrases are reinforced by the patterns of rhythm and sound. Robinson, the poet, is making his words give a total impression and have a total meaning, and all his devices contribute to this total effect.

A much more complicated poem is Shakespeare's sonnet number one. Not one of the best or best-known of his 154 sonnets, this poem still shows something of the complexity of sound, rhythm, and image patterns that can be found in lyric poetry:

> From fairest creatures we desire increase,
> that thereby beauty's rose might never die,
> 3   But as the riper should by time decease,
> His tender heir might bear his memory;
> But thou, contracted to thine own bright eyes,

6   Feed'st thy light's flame with self-substantial fuel,
    Making a famine where abundance lies,
    Thyself thy foe, to thy sweet self too cruel.
9   Thou that art now the world's fresh ornament
    And only herald to the gaudy spring,
    Within thine own bud buriest thy content
12 And, tender churl, mak'st waste in niggarding.
    Pity the world, or else this glutton be,
    To eat the world's due, by the grave and thee.

Like most sonnets, this poem is written in iambic pentameter lines; the first line, for instance, would probably best be scanned as

$$\overset{x}{\text{From fair}} \mid \overset{\prime}{\text{est crea}} \mid \overset{x}{\text{tures we}} \mid \overset{x}{\text{desire}} \mid \overset{x}{\text{increase.}}$$

As a so-called Shakespearean or English sonnet (as opposed to the Petrarchan or Italian type), its fourteen lines are organized in three groups of four lines each, called *quatrains,* with every other line of each quatrain rhyming. The three quatrains are followed by a *couplet* of rhyming lines. The first rhyme is *increase-decease* and is described as *a;* the next would be described as *b,* and so on, producing patterns of three quatrains and a couplet: *abab, cdcd, efef, gg.* What seems to be an inexact *b* rhyme of lines 2 and 4 is due largely to Shakespeare's having pronounced *die* differently from the way we do. After each quatrain a partial pause appears, but the main pause comes at the end of the third quatrain, line 12, setting off the couplet at the end from what has preceded it. The poem's thought is organized in terms of these divisions: quatrain 1, making a general statement about how we desire to perpetuate ourselves so as to keep from dying completely; quatrain 2, referring to a particular person who apparently acts against the principle described in the first four lines and does not try to perpetuate himself; quatrain 3, developing this idea, stating more clearly how this person's actions are destructive and opposed to the life principle of quatrain 1; and finally the couplet, taking off, as it were, from the twelve-line buildup. Beginning with a trochee, *pity,* that is also an imperative, the couplet plays against the basic iambic rhythm, stating, paradoxically as will be seen, what the person owes the world and what he should do to avoid being outside the life-force. The "solution" in this couplet is, however, hardly a developed statement. Being the conclusion of a build-up six times as long as it, the couplet must of necessity be suggestive and ambiguous, even paradoxical. This kind of sonnet is different from the Petrarchan or Italian kind, which has an eight-line development (the *octet* or *octave*) and a six-line resolution (the *sestet*), often producing a more symmetrical and balanced poem. But in this Shakespearean sonnet the couplet must bear the weight of everything that has gone before, and its two lines can only give a conclusion that contains elements of surprise and wonder.

The poem, one of several by Shakespeare on the general theme of procreation, points out that one owes it to oneself and the world to perpetuate one's beauty and merits. The production of offspring is thus seen as a form of immortality. But the poem is saying and doing much more than this statement of theme can possibly bring out. The poem is more than a clever statement to someone that he should propagate; whatever the particular occasion of the sonnet, it merits reading today because of its general significance, because it relates human beauty and love to all of nature, and because it shows this relationship in patterns of images and sounds that vitalize a common theme and that make us aware of life, death, beauty, time, and human responsibility in ways not previously realized.

The assonance and consonance here are much richer than in the relatively simple "Mr. Flood's Party." Certain ideas, not ordinarily obvious or compatible, are linked together through their sounds. The person addressed is one of the *f*airest creatures of line 1, but because he *f*eeds his *f*lame with *f*uel that ironically devours him (6), he creates a *f*amine out of the abundance (7). He himsel*f* is his *f*oe (8), he who now seems so *f*resh (9)—the word *fresh* returning us to the "fairest creatures" of line 1. Along with this [f] sound are a score of [s] and [z] sounds, running from fairest, creatures, desire, and increase in line 1 throughout the poem.

These, along with an [aI] vowel sound, as in desire, thereby, and die, decrease in quantity as the poem develops and are replaced in the later part by other vowels, such as [e]—waste, grave—and [ər]—buriest, churl—and by the stop consonants [b], [t], [g]—buriest, niggarding, glutton, grave, as well as by the nasals [n], [m], [ŋ]—thine, own, content, tender, mak'st, niggarding. These consonant sounds, [b], [m], and [n] in particular, appear early in the poem in such words as beauty and tender. It is hardly accidental that "beauty's rose" (2) and "bright eyes" (5) should lead to buriest (11), or that buriest should be preceded by bud, which refers back directly to "beauty's rose" and here shows the death that is, in a sense, denied in line 3.

The most interesting sound patterns in the poem are those like "bud buriest" (11) that by this similarity of sound force us to see certain words and ideas as related. All sorts of juxtapositions appear here that, as they make us uncomfortable, make us reevaluate the commonplace. Further instances of parallels and contrasts formed throughout the poem are "tender heir" in line 4, which is linked ironically to "tender churl" of line 12; increase (1) seen almost immediately in terms of decease (3); and the growth-death relationship which receives an increasingly paradoxical development—the constructive bear (1), meaning "carry on," becomes the destructive buriest (11), the irony coming about because of the sound similarity; similarly, feed'st (6) is linked with famine (7), in a sense its opposite; and this association is developed further at the end of the sonnet in waste (12), glutton (13), and eat (14). A similar ironic juxtaposition of terms that tend to be opposites is found in riper (3) and fresh (9), and in the statement that the person addressed, called "the world's fresh ornament" (9), devours himself, here expressed in "eat the world's due" (14). Beauty's rose, becoming riper, may live on through its heirs, as the first quatrain states; but as the third brings out, the person addressed

is fresh, in the spring of his life, and his bud is ironically being
destroyed without any rejuvenation or living on.

Something further of Shakespeare's artistry may be seen by
looking closely at two lines, the third and fourth for instance:

> But as the riper should by time decease,
> His tender heir might bear his memory;

As the final two lines of the first quatrain, they continue the
thought of the two preceding ones and may be paraphrased as
"Whereas the fairest of creatures ["beauty's rose"] will grow
older ["riper"] and ultimately die, it and its beauty might be
perpetuated through offspring." *Memory* stands for the qualities being passed on from one generation to the next; in bearing
his memory, the offspring are memorializing him. *Riper,* in the
comparative degree, gives a sense of the passing from youth to
old age and death; ripening leads to rotting, to what is created
here by the term *decease.* But *riper* through its ending comments also on *tender,* the two words being similar in form
though having meanings that tend to be opposites. Although
tender is not a comparative, the suggestion of mutability is given
to it, a suggestion reinforced by its alliteration with *time.*

But it is in line 4 that the sound patterns may best be seen:
heir and *bear* are linked in an internal rhyme of sorts, and
might and *memory* alliterate. Everything is held tightly together
like a wound-up spring that remains taut but is constantly tight-
ening and expanding as the poem develops. We become increasingly conscious of how it could burst apart; but although it
continually remains on the point of exploding, it amazingly
never does. This consciousness of what is held in and implied
increases as we reread the poem. Phrases, even terms, expand,
and the poem becomes an increasingly powerful statement.
Conciseness and rich connotation play against each other, creating for the sensitive reader an intense emotional and intellec-
tual experience.

Before concluding this chapter on the methods of the poem
it will be well to look once again at a work examined earlier.

We can now see that Pound's "In a Station of the Metro" is metrically constructed as follows:

$$\overset{x}{\text{The}}\ \overset{x}{\text{ap}} \mid \overset{x\ \prime}{\text{pari}} \mid \overset{x}{\text{tion}}\ \overset{x}{\text{of}} \mid \overset{x}{\text{these}}\ \overset{\prime}{\text{fa}} \mid \overset{x}{\text{ces}}\ \overset{x}{\text{in}} \mid \overset{x}{\text{the}}\ \overset{\prime}{\text{crowd}}:$$
$$\overset{\prime\ x}{\text{Petals}} \mid \overset{x\ x}{\text{on a}}\ \overset{\prime}{\text{wet,}} \mid \overset{\prime}{\text{black}}\ \overset{\prime}{\text{bough}}.$$

The first line is in six feet, hexameter, with alternating pyrrhics and iambs—though *these* may receive a half stress. The pattern of the many unstressed syllables punctuated by three stresses produces a staccato-like effect that contrasts with the movement of the second line. In three feet—a trochee, an anapest, and a spondee—it is half as long as the first and contains none of the metrical patterns found in the first. But at the same time it has the greater number of stresses and seems the more drawn out of the two. The first line lacks patterns of sound: the fricative *th* [ð] is the only noticeable one, and it exists only in unstressed syllables. But the second line is linked to it by means of the *p* sound of *apparition* and *petals,* words appearing early in their respective lines. The second line is also held together by the sound similarities of *pet*als and *wet* and by the alliteration of *black* and *bough.* Also these two sound patterns may be viewed as contrasting: the *p* and *t* consonants are voiceless stops and *b* is a voiced one. In fact, it appears as though the *p* sound, a voiceless labial stop, is changed in the line to the stronger *b,* its voiced equivalent.

Much more could be said about metrical and sound patterns in this poem and in verse in general, but what has been pointed out should be sufficient to indicate how important they are and how one can use them to understand something of the techniques and accomplishments of literature.

CHAPTER 6

Literary Content and Archetypal Themes

While it should be apparent by this time that in any work of poetry all elements contribute to the total meaning and effect, a point still needs to be clarified. We have been emphasizing the elements of form as though form were something different from and perhaps even more meaningful than content, the substance of the work. The relationship between form and content is one that is often not adequately understood. Often we tend to think of form as synonymous with artistry, with the art of literature itself, and content as that which has no real existence until it is formed. The literary artist in this view has been likened to the sculptor who takes an unformed chunk of rock and gives it a meaningful shape. The rock provides the sculptor with his material, but it does not become a piece of art until after it is chipped away and made into a certain shape.

Such may very well be the way content is in sculpture, but literature is another matter. It is a verbal, not a plastic, art; and words mean things apart from their artistic arrangement. The rock, the material of sculpture, is lifeless, but the content of literature—the story, the characters, even the words and rhythms themselves—are alive; and always in the case of the words, often in the case of the others, they are alive even before the artist uses them. Rather than be passively molded, they tend to mold themselves—as the modern playwright Luigi Pirandello realized and dramatized in *Six Characters in Search of an Author*. There a group of characters are trying to get their story told, and the literary artist is seen in a sense as their agent. He puts down on paper what is dictated by the story, the characters, and the idea. The content of literature is thus actively involved in the creation of literary works; as the contemporary poets Charles Olson and Robert Creely have phrased it, content seeks out its own form; form is never more than an extension of content.

The dividing line between the stuff of literature and its form is, to be sure, thin and difficult to see. Content and form overlap, and any separation we make of the two must be recognized as artificial, an after-the-fact way of examining what is in a work of art. If we are finally to see and understand what is there, we must view the work as though its form and content can be no other than what they are. There may be other sonnets on the subject of procreation and other versions of the narrative of Sir Patrick Spens, but when we are looking at Shakespeare's poem or the anonymous ballad quoted earlier, we find an integral relationship between content and form that makes these works different from any of the other versions. Should we leave out a stanza or a line, we no longer have the same poem. Similarly, should we do a prose rendition of the poem, we have something else. A horse of a different color is, in this sense at least, a different horse.

At the same time, it must be realized that any one story can be told in an almost endless variety of ways and that this story may reveal different themes according to the particular way it is told. One writer could, for instance, tell the tale of Sir Patrick Spens and make us feel that the mariner was foolish for following the king's commands; another could make the king seem like a wise and good man; still another could tell the story with the intention of trying to get better stabilizing equipment on ships so that they could navigate on the ocean in winter. Or, returning to "In a Station of the Metro," a poet other than Pound could take the same subject and make us despise the lonely faces in the crowd, or use the subject to make a statement condemning modern life as dehumanizing. The Hamlet story, for instance, existed in world literature for centuries before Shakespeare wrote his version of it, using the material in a particular artistic way and creating the powerful, compelling drama we know. There are likewise scores of stories about the Trojan War, about Faustus who sold his soul to the devil for knowledge, about King Arthur and his Knights of the Round Table who searched for the Holy Grail, and about the lover Don Juan. In each case the particular author has formed the subject into a particular creation of his own; but at the same time each story may be said to contain something compelling to people in all times and places, something that makes all the particular formings of it substantial and meaningful. The choice of an immortal plot does not, of course, guarantee that the resulting composition will be substantial or meaningful but only that its chances are that much better.

Also the content itself often has significations of its own that may be overlooked or misunderstood by its particular formers. But even when a writer does not intend certain significations, they often appear because they reside in the subject. The expression of the subject may, of necessity, bring them out; and they may at times color, slant, or just get in the way of the particular treatment and its author's points. Sometimes a writer has a particular thesis which he tries to impose on or, more legitimately, bring out of his material. But his thesis may not be totally compatible with the material, or the content may contain built-in themes more striking and more pertinent than the theme the writer is trying to develop.

One of the most compelling, most popular stories in the Western world is that of Oedipus, king of Thebes, known best today through the version by the ancient Greek dramatist Sophocles. But the story itself, the content of Sophocles' play,

existed as a well-known legend long before Sophocles wrote in
the fifth century B.C. Sophocles ordered his material in such a
way as to produce a great drama, but some of his themes and
motifs represent significances found in the content of the legend.
A couple of illustrations will show what I mean. Determined in
his pride and self-confidence to find the man who killed King
Laius and brought the curse of the gods to Thebes, Oedipus
blindly hurtles along, unaware that he himself is the sinner. In
killing Laius, he killed his own father, and in marrying Laius'
widow, Jocasta, he married his own mother. But at one point
in Oedipus' pursuit of the truth, he begins to worry. Jocasta,
his mother-wife, telling him the story of Laius' death, mentions
that the king was killed at a place where three roads meet.
At these words Oedipus is troubled. In the translation of E. F.
Watling what occurs next reads as follows:

Oedipus: My wife, what you have said has troubled me.
My mind goes back . . . and something in me moves . . .

Jocasta: Why? What is the matter? How you turn and start!

Oedipus: Did you not say that Laius was killed
At a place where three roads meet?

Jocasta: That was the story;
And is the story still.

Oedipus: Where? In what country?

Jocasta: The land called Phocis—where the road divides,
Leading to Delphi and to Paulia.

Oedipus: How long ago did it happen?

Jocasta: It became known
A little time before your reign began.

Oedipus: O God, what wilt thou do to me!

And the dialogue continues, full of Oedipus' fear and sense of foreboding as he remembers that, while on his way to Thebes, he himself killed a man "at a place where three roads meet." In the subsequent lines Oedipus is determined more than ever to find out what really happened, a seeking that finally results in the realization of his own guilt and his downfall. But the focus at this point in the drama is on the "place where three roads meet."

In ancient times crossroads were significant, because it was unusual for one highway to cross another outside a town. Such places were often shrines and were viewed as having a supernatural significance. It was even more unusual and significant for *three* roads to cross one another; there must have been few such spots in ancient Greece. The road-crossing in Sophocles' play seems to contain an ancient, half-forgotten significance; and as the reference to it pushes into Oedipus' consciousness, making him remember and suspect, it comes to have a special existence of its own. The "place where three roads meet" haunts his mind, and he is insecure for the first time in Sophocles' play. Igor Stravinsky, the twentieth-century composer, makes a similar, even more dramatic use of this detail from the legend. In his opera-oratorio version of the Oedipus story, as Oedipus hears Jocasta speak of where Laius was killed, the chorus begins a haunting phrase, repeating *trivium* (a Latin word meaning "three roads") over and over. The sound drives itself into Oedipus's consciousness and becomes something like his heartbeat. Throughout Oedipus' anxious words that follow, the beat and the haunting sound continue.

The composer and the dramatist, though living twenty-five centuries apart, were able to use in individual ways a detail of the myth. They made dramatically and psychologically meaningful something that has now lost the particular significance it once had in the legend. Perhaps the three roads crossing represented something both sacred and supernatural, and when Oedipus killed a man—a king and his own father, no less—at the crossing, he not only committed murder, patricide, and regicide, but also violated the particular-place taboo. In any case, what can be seen is that Sophocles and Stravinsky found this detail meaningful and were able to use it to help make their versions of the Oedipus story powerful and compelling.

In this instance an element of content was able to assert itself through the particular forming it took, but not all motifs fare so well. One content motif lost in Sophocles' *Oedipus Rex* and not really found and understood until the advent of Freudian psychoanalysis in the twentieth century allowed man to rediscover the symbolic significance of certain details. In Sophocles' play, after realizing the enormity of his sins and crimes, Oedipus tears his eyes out with great pins. In the words of the attendant who reports this action to the people on stage,

> He pierced his eyeballs time and time again,
> Till bloody tears ran down his breast—not drops
> But in full spate, a whole cascade descending
> In drenching cataracts of scarlet rain.

When Jocasta, his mother-wife, realized that she had married her son, she killed herself. But Oedipus, as Sophocles presents the story, seems to think blinding himself a sufficient and fitting self-punishment. As the attendant reports, Oedipus thrusts the pins into his eyes,

> Eyes that should see no longer his shame, his guilt,
> No longer see those they should never have seen
> Nor see, unseeing, those he had longed to see,
> Henceforth seeing nothing but night . . .

But in spite of the paradoxical language there appears to be a noticeable inadequacy here. Oedipus' action of blinding himself so that he will not have to look on his shame seems less appropriate than Jocasta's suicide as a punishment for the sin. Freudian psychology suggests a built-in symbolic significance of the blinding—castration, which would be a terribly fitting punishment for one who has committed incest.

Rather than use the blindness to suggest castration, Sophocles makes it meaningful and functional by using it as the climax of the idea of seeing and not-seeing that he develops throughout his play. The intricate pattern of images having to do with sight and blindness acquires meaning from this scene, and the theme of the play becomes fuller and clearer. At the beginning of the drama, when he possessed physical sight, Oedipus was blind to his own sins and to what had occurred. He even berated and mocked Tiresias, the old blind seer who, though without eyesight, possessed insight. At this point in the play the contrast between Tiresias and Oedipus is clear, and when Oedipus later blinds himself, he is, as it were, closing his eyes to the world and looking within. He has started to gain consciousness, to become like Tiresias; now, ironically, for the first time, Oedipus is a see-er.

This contrast of images, this play on seeing and not-seeing, is a conscious dramatic device that Sophocles is bringing to his material. The contrast may reside within his material, but the images certainly do not function there with the artistry and paradoxical significance he gives them. It must still be emphasized, however, that his artistic control is, in this instance at least, at the expense of the symbolic castration, which seems to have been the point of the blindness in the traditional story. That is, Oedipus' blinding himself is made by Sophocles to fit integrally into an artistic pattern he has created; but had he been aware of, and able to use, the castration idea already existing in his content, his dramatic and psychological presentation might have been all the greater.

In early Western literature—old English narratives, ancient Irish sagas, medieval vernacular romances and ballads, as well as folk and fairy tales—the mythic material often comes through the "literary" treatment it has been given by a particular teller. Sometimes this mythic material is garbled, sometimes the writer seems to have been aware of its existence but has not known what to do with it; but frequently its significance is so compelling, the material so strong, that it comes to the surface in spite of not being consciously used. When, however, a writer tries to keep his content from going its own way and his themes from receiving the expression they insist on receiving, he is like the cook who tries to keep warm yeast from rising, a task both impossible and unproductive. He may also be compared to the gardener who plants petunias in a bed of lily bulbs. Whether the gardener knows it or not, the lilies are already in the ground, and they will most likely come up, probably even getting in the way of the petunias. When he returns to his patch of land, he may be surprised at what has come of his planting.

One of the most striking illustrations of just such a failure to recognize and use content is Virgil's *Aeneid*. Working with the traditional and legendary content of the Trojan War, Virgil did not allow his material to develop itself and exhibit its own values and meanings. Rather, he was concerned wholly with using it to bring out certain qualities in his hero, Aeneas, and to create his "great theme" of the founding of Rome. One of the few Trojans to escape from Troy, Aeneas is destined for a great purpose. Guided by his mother, the goddess Venus (his father was a mortal), Aeneas journeys through the Mediterranean world exhibiting the virtues Virgil prized, and finally goes to Italy to found what will become the Roman empire. As Virgil presents him, Aeneas is characterized by the Latin term *pius*—here meaning "good, worthy, and noble"—and in his adventures after the fall of Troy he continually moves away from the earthly world of the senses. The flesh is for Virgil imperfect, emotion or passion is a weakness, and the ideal man is he who can escape the storms and passions of the senses. Aeneas journeys to become the man of reason; with his descent to Hades, his purification is complete in one sense of the word, and he is eligible to found the great empire of Rome, seen by Virgil as the perfection of human actions and the earthly paradise itself.

Perhaps the best way of understanding how Virgil has wrenched his material and tried to make it fit the themes he has in mind is to compare the end of his poem with that of Homer's *Odyssey*. Homer was a model for Virgil, but the

Odyssey and the *Iliad* are really very different from Virgil's *Aeneid.* In the last part of the *Odyssey,* after being tested and proved in the world of the supernatural, Odysseus returns to the human world, here Ithaca, to set his household and state in order—an act comparable to Aeneas' coming to Italy to found Rome but yet one that is in actuality quite different from that in the *Aeneid.* Aeneas sweeps before him those deluded persons who are bound by passion, those who like Dido and Turnus rage and act rashly; and at the conclusion of the poem there is to be no ambiguity, no doubt in our mind that the better man has won and that a new great day is dawning for the world. In Aeneas' victory over Turnus we are to see that reason has been all-victorious and that man has now reached a new point in life.

At the end of the *Odyssey,* on the other hand, all is ambiguous. Returning to Ithaca, Odysseus must kill the suitors who have been wasting his property, desiring his wife, and scheming for control of his kingdom. But his fight with them is like a slaughter. Odysseus' actions—like those of wrathful Achilles in the *Iliad*—are excessive and terrible; they hardly signify perfection of character. But character perfection does not seem to be Homer's purpose. Whereas Virgil tries to wrap up everything in a nice package and tie it with a bow, Homer leaves ends dangling and parts not enclosed. This does not represent a weakness in the *Odyssey* but rather a sense that "solutions" are not necessarily the most desirable thing. Rather than end as the *Aeneid* does with a final victory, the *Odyssey* continues beyond the fighting. Following the massacre of the suitors, Odysseus finds that he must cope with the relatives of the men he has killed, and it looks as though the slaughter will continue. The work ends, and we are able to see beyond the conflict, only because the goddess of reason, Pallas Athene, comes down to earth to stop the fighting. But except for the wanderings of Odysseus, nothing is really concluded at the end of this narrative. Homer has not given us—as Virgil has—the answers, the solutions, to life; if anything, he has made us aware of its ambiguities.

Virgil's idea in his poem has been to present a particular point or "message," not to allow his material to demonstrate its own meaning. He took preexisting material, but rather than let this content grow as an organic entity, he imposed his own themes and forms on it. To express this in another way, Virgil took traditionally mythic material—most directly from the *Iliad* and the *Odyssey* and the legends of Troy—but then wrenched this material to make it fit the special purposes he had in mind. It is possible to see, for example, how the wanderings of Aeneas parallel those of Odysseus, how Aeneas' victory over Turnus is like Achilles' over Hector; but there is a marked difference in what Virgil and Homer are doing in their works. The two authors show very different views of literature. In Homer the epic appears as a heroic narrative centering on the human: it is a celebration of man in all his imperfection and glory. In Virgil, on the other hand, the epic takes on a sense of purpose or mission: it reveals what the good man must be like and how a great empire was founded. Before he is a writer Virgil is a patriot and a moralist. He wants to memorialize the grand origins of his state and tries to show the citizens of Rome the kind of person they must be if Rome is to keep its greatness.

But the main trouble with Virgil's scheme is that it does not wholly work. Even though the author's intention seems to be, for instance, that we condemn Dido for her excesses of passion, especially for her rash act of killing herself, Dido is for us a flesh-and-blood human being whom we like and respect in many ways more than we do Aeneas. Similarly, though we are certainly not supposed to, we may find ourselves sympathizing with Turnus—as we do with Hector in the *Iliad*. But whereas in the *Iliad* our sympathies are acceptable—Homer himself seems to have admired the Trojan leader—in Virgil's view it is wrong, even perverse, for us to feel pity for the adversary of the noble Aeneas. While we may acknowledge Virgil's aims, we should still recognize that after he gets through using his material, something remains that does not quite fit in with what he is doing. The organic life of the content is still there, though pushed down by the hand of the conscious literary artist, here historian and moralist, who, like someone wearing blinders, writes with but a single intention in mind.

One way of understanding how content functions is to understand how certain themes permeate literature and how these themes link various works often disparate on the surface. To regard the variations of the theme is often to understand how the theme functions in a particular work, and to understand the theme of one work in terms of the same theme in others is to be further aware of both the particular accomplishment represented by the individual work and the nature of literature. One such theme, limited enough to be presented here, is that of the outcast.

From the earliest literature of the Western world to the most recent contemporary writings, the outcast has been prominent as a striking and compelling character and idea. Although found in such peripheral forms as Robinson Crusoe, the castaway who lives as a hermit apart from the world, the real outcast is the human being who has detached himself from the group or who has been detached from the group because of his views or actions. This figure, the man detached from, and perhaps even challenging, the ordered processes of society, is one that frequently calls up in us a sympathetic response. But such a response has not always been the usual one. Traditionally, the outcast is by definition the person who has been driven out of his society and civilization. His being condemned to banishment is almost the equivalent of his being condemned to death. The man ostracized from his fellowmen exists, as it were, apart from the world order. He has been driven out of the light into the darkness, and he finds himself in the midst of a chaos that is without relief for him.

Although today the man without a country is no fearful creature, he is seen traditionally as one to be pitied and abhorred. Such a response may be due to the traditional view that one's being is determined by the group or society with which he is identified. As long as that particular society exists, so does the individual; but once the society is destroyed, the individual loses his own reason for being. One's obligation is customarily to the group and the ruler of the group—king, feudal lord, or whatever he may be. If one does not fulfill this obligation—if, for example, one puts his own good against the general good—he thereby commits the crime of treason and, as it were, negates his own being. To approach this idea from another point of view, one's own views and desires should coincide with those of the society of which one is a member. When they coincide, there exists a condition of general peace and harmony; when, however, the individual and the common good are opposed, trouble is bound to come.

A formalization of this idea takes place in the Christian Middle Ages, especially in the fifth century with St. Augustine's idea of charity and cupidity. *Charity* may be defined as the kind of love that is unselfish, that exists not for the particular good of the individual but for the general good. It is directed outward, aimed at serving and helping others. In its customary form it is love of neighbors and God. *Cupidity,* on the other hand, is the opposite of this outgoing, all-embracing, constructive, and ordering love. Based on love of self, it is present when one puts one's own well-being ahead of the general good. It is not love at all but rather lust or inordinate, self-destroying passion.

The person whose behavior is marked by cupidity is the outcast, if for no other reason than because of his state of mind. In this sense *outcast* is implicitly the same as *rebel.* The man who challenges the existing order may be, in the world view that developed from Hellenic times, a heroic figure—even the Promethean figure who chooses to be the outlaw and outcast because of what he believes to be right. We tend to admire the rebel, whether he finally suffers for his beliefs or whether he is ultimately brought back into the society he challenged, as with the figure of Robin Hood. At the same time, however, our response to the outcast as rebel is one of grateful relief. We may envy him his unique characteristics, but still we feel glad that it is he and not we who exist as the outcast. In this sense the outcast is a projection of our desires and a scapegoat for our fears.

Nevertheless, the rebel, generally marked by pride, is ordinarily different from the man of charity. This ideal man is best illustrated by the Judaic-Christian hero who passively accepts whatever happens to him. The figure of Job, for example, is more than rebel. Although he initially questions and challenges, he ultimately accepts. This acceptance is what brings him back into the world order, what gives the Book of Job its "happy ending," and what makes Job in effect the hero. Similarly, the figure of Samson, as in Milton's *Samson Agonistes,* goes beyond being the outcast, because Samson finally repents of his pride. He is thus able to be strong again and, most important, to be God's servant again. In this view, rather than project and assert oneself, one must hold back and realize that "They also serve who only stand and wait."

When this passive accepter becomes the ideal, the rebel is deprecated; he may even become a projection of the archrebel Satan. To rebel and choose to become the outcast is in this view to choose evil. The descendants of Prometheus thus tend to become the descendants of the devil. Both Prometheus and Satan challenged the gods, but the two figures are very different—at least in the responses they cause in us. Specifically, Prometheus is a tragic hero, the main character, in fact, of several dramas; but Satan is wholly a villain. Both were punished for their presumption, but while there is a grandeur in Prometheus' persevering while his liver is gnawed eternally by vultures, there is only a degradation in Satan's being hurled to hell. Prometheus stole fire from the gods to help man, but Satan merely wanted to elevate himself over God and the angels. In his pride he acts as the archetype of cupidity and exists to show men what happens to those who challenge the existing order, especially the existing divine order. He is designed to be a figure of horror.

Human counterparts to Satan in the Judaic-Christian tradition are such figures as Cain, the Wandering Jew, and Faust. These are rebels who have chosen to break away from the good; they have sinned and been punished, but there is something fascinating about them for us. While they and their crimes may be lacking in the dignity of Prometheus and his defiance, we still regard them with awe, probably because of their punishment and their mere act of defiance. We know that insofar as they exist for our edification, we are to regard them as "evil," but at the same time they are more than this. Perhaps our fascination with them is based on a desire we may have to do what is forbidden. These men have murdered, blasphemed, and sold their souls to the devil. They have done what most of us would never dare to do or even dare to want to do. We are horrified by them and their crimes, but we are also attracted. These men are outcasts and criminals; but even though our Judaic-Christian heritage demands that we condemn them, we still view them as titans.

We might even relate our feelings about these figures to our response to Job. The most compelling thing about Job is not his "patience," as the term is usually understood, or his ultimate understanding, but, rather, his cursing himself and challenging the world order to give a reason for his suffering. The rebel wants to alter the status quo; Satan, Prometheus, Faust, and Job are all threats to what exists. But it is the outcome of their rebellion, not the rebellion itself, that really determines our response. That is, if the rebel is successful in his rebellion and achieves his end, he is no longer rebel but, rather, ruler of a new world order. If he is unsuccessful, he becomes more than rebel too; he becomes the outcast. A state of mind becomes a physical condition.

It is rare that an outcast can ever return to the existing world order without destroying it or changing his own point of view, but such a return can and does happen in the story of Oedipus that Sophocles tells. At the end of *Oedipus Rex* Oedipus is explicitly the outcast. Shunned and abhorred by both men and gods for his unintentional incest and patricide, he is homeless, friendless, sightless. Led out of Thebes by his young daughters, Oedipus is at the end of this play a figure in many ways to be pitied. In the sequel, *Oedipus at Colonnus,* however, Oedipus is revealed once again as the great hero. His elevation comes about not because of any penance he has done, not because he has repented of his crimes, but because he has continually challenged the gods for causing him to do what he unknowingly did. Oedipus will not accept the blame; in his view what happened to him was unjust. Ultimately the gods come to agree with Oedipus, and he is elevated to paradise, becoming something of a god himself.

The outcast is usually, however, a figure who remains apart from the world order. Instead of being an Everyman figure, he may be viewed, in effect, as a scapegoat for Everyman, a sacrificial victim to exonerate Average Man from his own antisocial crimes and tendencies. Even Oedipus had to be driven out so that Thebes could once again thrive. It seems that society both demands a scapegoat and produces one in its figure of the outcast. One of the most extreme statements of the necessity of creating a scapegoat-outcast appears in Shirley Jackson's short story "The Lottery." Here the selection of the sacrificial victim, who is a priori the outcast, is a formalized, ritualized event, occurring annually as part of the life of the society presented in the story. The most frightening thing about this selection is its festive atmosphere, its implication that nothing out of the ordinary is happening as the victim is stoned to death. The woman who is victim in no way deserves what happens to her, except as she is a member of society. She is the victim simply because there must be a victim. The implication is that if the victim is not provided, society will not function properly.

The outcast as mere victim, though perhaps necessary to

the world, lacks the grandeur and power of a Cain or Faust; he is more pathetic than tragic, and we feel sorry for him rather than admire him. Such outcasts are hardly to be separated from those who are merely the victims of life. Such a "common" outcast is Willy Loman in Arthur Miller's play *Death of a Salesman*. Willy is principally a *low man,* a term that may suggest a common man, but one that means more precisely a man brought low or reduced by the world. For his whole life Willy Loman has been a producing, useful member of his society. When he becomes old and cannot function as a member of this society, it is essential—for the good of the society—that he be removed. But his removal—that is, his becoming an outcast—has all sorts of complications resulting from the fact that Willy is a human being, and human beings have feelings. These complications are at the heart of Miller's play. But no matter how much Miller discusses and analyzes Willy's problem, the problem is still not resolved. The pathetic thing at the end of the play is that Willy is presented as a hero, specifically as an ideal, and that at least one of Willy's sons is going to follow in his father's footsteps and "fight the good fight." Here the mere fight seems to be held up as something wholly good in itself, containing its own justification and rewards.

When we speak of the ironic victim, we are not talking about just one kind of person. As Northrop Frye points out, we should distinguish between two kinds of ironic victims. The first is, like Adam, the man who is destined to be the victim; he can only fall, and he must fall. His whole existence is, as it were, to fall. The second and more interesting kind is what Frye terms the incongruously ironic victim, the man who, like Christ, does not deserve everything that happens to him. It is often through being the ironic victim, especially the incongruously ironic kind, that the individual is able to become the hero.

It is customary for the potential hero to be lowered—humbled or humiliated—and to leave the world of his familiar existence. He must prove himself apart from what he knows, and he can use only his own courage, prowess, and wisdom in this test. In fact, it may be said that his separation, his state of "apartness," is what enables him to attain and reveal his worth. Just as Christ's forty days in the wilderness were essential to him, so Hamlet's separation from both his past—his school days and friends—and his present —the life of the Danish court—is necessary for him. Hamlet is the outcast because of his feeling that something is wrong, and also because of his need to understand what he is doing. To act and not to think is easy; what Hamlet must do is neither easy nor popular. It is not the way of the world. When one becomes the outcast, no matter what particular kind of outcast, one becomes, of necessity, different from one's fellows. One often becomes, as it were, the oddball, regarded, at least in part, with suspicion and general hostility.

It is significant, however, that in recent literature the hero is more an outcast than ever. He may be, like Holden Caulfield in J. D. Salinger's *Catcher in the Rye* or Ralph in William Golding's *Lord of the Flies,* a confused and ineffectual youth protesting against the brutalizing ways of the world. Or he may be, like Jacob Horner in John Barth's *End of the Road* and the title figure in Saul Bellow's *Herzog,* a man unable to rise above being a loser. But he is still marked by a consciousness, even a dignity, that makes him different from his fellowmen. The dominant characteristics, however, of these stories with hero-victims are ambiguity and irony. The main characters are often weak and helpless, and when they are not, they are apt to be like Sebastian Dangerfield in J. P. Donleavy's *Ginger Man*—selfish, irresponsible, cruel, and vicious, but possessing a sense of humor that is their only redeeming trait.

Stories about these figures usually lack the catharsis found in tradition tragedy, the good humor of comedy where things turn out well, and even the bitterness of irony where waste is the norm. They are, rather, demonstrations of the "absurd" and frequently exhibit what has been termed "black humor." Lost in a world that is basically irrational and destructive, the outcasts in contemporary fiction are most often destroyed and, Hemingway notwithstanding, also defeated. While we can only laugh or cry at the irony and absurdity of it all and feel how ridiculous these figures and their situations are, we still—and this is the greatest irony of all—tend to identify more with the outcasts than with the victorious world and its dubious values. The outcast may seem to be an absurd hero, but he is increasingly the only kind of hero we know or can accept. The theme of the outcast may thus be seen as a pattern inherent in a certain content and developed in different ways by various writers.

There are, of course, many other patterns in literature; but there are also other kinds of patterns. One of these may be described as a structuring pattern, one giving shape and direction to content and its themes. An example of such a structuring pattern is the motif of the journey. Without being primarily concerned with a classification of journey motifs, we can see how the journey functions in various narratives.

As a term denoting genre, the journey is traditionally linked to those works of fiction described as picaresque, those, of which Henry Fielding's *Tom Jones* is a notable example, that have as their setting a continual change in scenery, a wandering not integrally related to character development but used as a focal point for plot. When this journey is in time rather than in space, it shows a character growing older and maturing and produces the kind of narrative often termed a *Bildungsroman*. Novels of this sort are Charles Dickens' *David Copperfield* and James Joyce's *Portrait of the Artist as a Young Man*. In both the picaresque novel and the *Bildungsroman*, in spite of differences between the types and among the individual works within the types, the journey functions as an overall device giving unity, direction, and even a particular atmosphere.

Sometimes the spatial or temporal journey is used both as

a means of developing plot and character and as a way of revealing a thematic or psychological journey. In such works as Melville's *Moby Dick* and Homer's *Odyssey* the specific journey has a symbolic purpose of revealing an additional dimension. While having a reality of its own, while being concrete and realistically detailed, the kind of journey seen in these works contains within itself implications and meanings that make it ultimately more than it seems at first. Related to this kind of symbolic journey is the allegorical one, the kind that acts as the basis of such works as John Bunyan's *Pilgrim's Progress,* Edmund Spenser's *Faerie Queene,* and, in part, Dante's *Divine Comedy.* The differences between the allegorical and symbolic journeys are very much like the differences discussed earlier between allegory and symbolism, and even a superficial comparison of, say, *Pilgrim's Progress* and *Moby Dick* makes the differences apparent. Christian's journey in Bunyan's work has no reality of its own. Anchored to nothing tangible, it exists merely to stand for an abstract journey within the self; and we see that, although the journey is a symbol of sorts, Bunyan relies on the reader's giving it a meaning it lacks in itself. In *Pilgrim's Progress* the reader must translate the journey and its machinery into the terms he knows the writer wants and take the lesson he knows the writer wants to bring out. *Moby Dick,* however, reveals a journey that is of this world at the same time that it suggests forces above the familiar and the natural.

Related to the use of one journey as a symbol for another still larger one is the use of two actual journeys, one, as it were, inside the other. In such a work as John Steinbeck's *Grapes of Wrath* we find several inner chapters which herald and enlarge upon the westward journey of the Joad family and which transform the specific journey of this family into something much larger and more universal than the particular account of a family of Oakies moving to California. These chapters-within-chapters act as a journey in microcosm and also present a movement that relates to and plays on the main narrative movement of the book. The figural relationship—in Erich Auerbach's terms—that is created by this interplay acts as a structuring principle giving form to the entire novel. The relationship may be seen by looking at the early inner chapters that show a turtle trying to cross Route 66. The turtle's effort is linked to the Oakies' travels, and, at the same time, the turtle's troubles forecast and suggest the imminent problems and frustrations in store for the Joads and for all the other Oakies along the way.

Finally, we may see the journey as an overall allegory of life. In journeys of this sort (like that found in E. M. Forster's short story "The Other Side of the Hedge") we see the outward trip and the return on the metaphorical road of life—a road that begins where it ends and yet, in going around and around in twisting circles, still gives the impression of leading somewhere. This journey to nowhere provides the author with his vehicle for commenting on life and on man's continual striving to get ahead.

Relevant as such classifications may be, there are still other ways of looking at the journey and its role in literature. Rather than continuing to analyze kinds of journeys, let us synthesize them. The journey outward, the journey to adventure, new discoveries, and new lands, whether spatial, temporal, or symbolic in any way, may be regarded as a quest. On this journey we find the hero in the midst of life, meeting obstacles of all sorts which he always overcomes, and there is never any real fear in our mind that he will do otherwise. The quest is not found too often as the entire narrative in literature because by its very nature it emphasizes action rather than character or the relationship between the action at hand and the person involved in it. In popular writing that appeals because of its narrative level, quests seem ever-present, existing wholly to entertain. No matter whether in the form of a Western, a historical war story, or a medieval romance, these works look much the same, exhibiting the same motifs, characters, and resolutions; the names and styles are the only things that vary from work to work.

In all stories of quests the appeal is one of external excitement, of danger. But it is an unreal, a pretended danger, for we all know that the hero will win the day, conquer his adversaries, and appear at the end, if not unscathed, at least undaunted and ready for more adventures. In more sophisticated handlings of the quest motif, however—in such a work as Homer's *Odyssey*—action is subordinated to character rather than the other way around. Odysseus is not to be seen as the agent of the action; he is more real and more important than what he does, and what he does refers to our understanding of him. His journeys are exciting narratives in themselves, but they function mainly as the substance of his struggle to return to Ithaca and the means of his developing consciousness.

Opposed to the quest, though similar to it in some ways, is what may be termed the pilgrimage. If the quest is the journey outward to external adventure, the pilgrimage is the journey inward, one involving self-understanding. Rather than entertain by presenting a hero who conquers external obstacles, the pilgrimage generally shows a moral rise or a new awareness in the main character and acts to teach us what we ourselves should do. When seen in an isolated state, it, like the quest, is generally somewhat subliterary—though one of the best examples of the pilgrimage per se is *Pilgrim's Progress,* a work revealing in the guise of an actual physical pilgrimage a true pilgrimage of the human spirit.

Such a pilgrimage can also be found in the *Divine Comedy,* where we, along with Dante, are led down through Hell. Then, as we learn of and go beyond deadly sin, we ascend the mount of Purgatory; and finally, after being purified and reaching a state of consciousness and grace, we attain Paradise. At the beginning of the work, however, Dante—the narrator and the main character—finds himself in the middle of the journey of life, lost in a dark wood. The distinct implication is that Dante had been on another journey but found himself sidetracked from it. The journey that takes him ultimately to Paradise is apparently a different one. Similarly, in Book I of the *Faerie Queene,* the Red Cross Knight and Una make a journey that cannot be successful until the knight achieves a purification he is lacking. His subsequent education in the House of Holiness acts as a pilgrimage, a progress through the rites of purification, that enables him to reach the heavenly city and fulfill his worldly quest.

Even in such plainly didactic works as these, we find the pilgrimage—the inward seeking for an understanding of self combined with the quest—the outward searching for adventures and worldly glory. The combination not only gives a full picture of human endeavor, the pilgrimage completing in a sense what was begun by the quest, but may result in an artistic whole, since the pilgrimage tends to emphasize character and theme while the quest stresses narrative action. Furthermore, the combination presents a narrative level which is of interest in itself, and a thematic or symbolic level which gives meaning to the narrative level. In a work like the Middle English *Sir Gawain and the Green Knight,* for example, we have a very real combination of story and meaning. Gawain, prince of knights, proudest and best of Arthur's court, exists initially in terms of the world of outward adventure and meets a series of obstacles and temptations; but at the end we find that the actions have really been a series of tests and that the whole purpose of the actions has been to give Gawain an understanding of himself, his faults and merits, and to aid him in reaching a moral elevation.

To look at the quest and the pilgrimage in a slightly different way, we find not only that one completes the other but also that the main character, having the experience of one, needs the experience of the other as well. Thus, Dante's journey to perfection through understanding and experiencing Hell, Purgatory, and Paradise is as meaningful as it is partly because Dante has come to this pilgrimage from an earlier, less satisfactory journey. Likewise in Book I of the *Faerie Queene,* the Red Cross Knight is first the quester and then the pilgrim. He can exist and conquer in one world, but to attain any real or spiritual victory he must be able to do more than recognize the dragon Error. Consequently, his pilgrimage enables him to develop so as to be fully prepared for both this world and the next. In *Sir Gawain and the Green Knight,* the quest and the pilgrimage exist not as two chronologically contiguous episodes but as one superimposed on the other. For example, when Gawain goes to find the Green Chapel so that the Green Knight can chop off his head and thus pay him back for his earlier blow, he fights all sorts of wild animals, giants, and monsters along the way, and wards off a tempting lady as well. These adventures, on the surface those of a quest, are essential for the pilgrimage that Gawain is also making in that they determine his fate and act as the means of giving him insight.

It remains to discuss one or two works in greater detail using what has been said so far of the journey and the journeyer. In Mark Twain's *Huckleberry Finn* we find not only a journey in time and space but a vivid use of the combined quest-pilgrimage archetypes. On his raft voyage along the Mississippi River, Huck acts as the quester: he has all sorts of adventures, meets and overcomes obstacles, and is involved in all the problems and ugliness of life. It is probably to Huck's adventures and conquests that the reader—especially the adolescent reader—first responds, and there is no denying that there is an appeal here. Huck, an adolescent himself, can easily be identified with, and his adventures away from stifling civilization are exciting in themselves and are of the sort that might exist in the daydreams of one not so free as Huck.

At the same time Huck exists as a pilgrim: he receives a new understanding of life and of his role in it. This is not to say that he is conscious of his role, but we can easily observe the change in him by the time his combined quest-pilgrimage is over. At the end, when Huck is brought into contact with Tom Sawyer, it is clear that he is no longer the child he was earlier. Tom's games seem inane both to Huck and to us. The way Tom goes about freeing the slave Jim, for example, is shown to be that of a child having a child's adventure. Huck, on the other hand, does not have to play, for he has had dangerous and real adventures. These have been integrally involved in developing his new awareness of life.

The journey along the river thus combines within itself both quest and pilgrimage, and Huck contains the quester and the pilgrim within himself. The outward, external life is revealed strikingly as the story develops, but the book is more than a travelogue of life on the Mississippi. We, as well as Mark Twain, are interested less in the events themselves than in the effect they have on the young journeyer. But for the events of the external world to be meaningfully handled, the boy must first develop himself. Twain does not stop the voyage along the river to show Huck going off on a spiritual pilgrimage. Time is not suspended while, through coping with a different set of problems, like the Red Cross Knight in the *Faerie Queene,* Huck prepares himself for meeting the problems of this world. Rather, we find—as was the case in *Sir Gawain and the Green Knight*—that the pilgrimage is superimposed on the quest, one really becoming the other. The boy's outward adventures thus become the inward adventures; the experiences of life become those that develop his character. The external life is then a vehicle for theme, showing Huck's progress; and the novel, more than a Pilgrim's Progress, may be seen as a Pilgrim's and Quester's Progress. The only thing wrong with using *Huckleberry Finn* for illustration is that one might think the quest-pilgrimage is a priori a maturation. This may in part be so, but the reverse statement has no validity: the maturation process found throughout literature is never a priori the quest-pilgrimage.

To counteract *Huckleberry Finn,* as well as to show the other side of the coin, we may look once again at *Moby Dick.* In this novel we find our interest divided primarily between story and character. First, we want to know what will be the result of the *Pequod's* voyage, what will happen when the ship and the white whale meet; and second, we find ourselves becoming increasingly fascinated with Captain Ahab. But these two elements of interest are very much related to each other, because they are the journey that is being made and the journeyer who is making it. And in these terms it is significant that the story is being told by a character named Ishmael, an archetypal wanderer.

The journey here is not a simple one. In the terms we have been using, it combines the quest and the pilgrimage, but only in relation to the Ahab who makes this particular voyage. The Ahab of the earlier whale hunts—apparently quite different, outwardly at least, from the Ahab of this one—seems to have been primarily concerned with whale hunting as a business and as an adventure. But now that he has lost his leg to the white whale, the whole purpose of his life has changed. The journey has been given meaning by the journeyer, but Ahab is the combined quester-pilgrim in an inverted sense. Apparently seeking after life, he, maimed in mind and body, is pursuing death—an ambiguity likewise revealed in the white whale, especially in the chapter called "The Whiteness of the Whale." Melville makes us conscious of the opposing forces combined in the whale—good and bad, creator and destroyer, god and devil—and the same ambiguity is found in Ahab and his quest. As white in the whale suggests both innocence and death, so does the dark figure of Ahab suggest both evil and wronged innocence. On his journey Ahab is both the quester who is trying to conquer an opponent and the pilgrim who is trying to find himself. The great irony here is that the only thing conquered is Ahab himself, and all that is found is death and emptiness. Rather than reveal any increased consciousness or moral rise, Ahab shows a moral degeneration and even becomes what he was trying to destroy. He is at the end the destroyer who has dragged down with him his entire crew save one. Whereas the end of the journey in *Huckleberry Finn* is re-creation, development of the journeyer, the end in *Moby Dick* is destruction. In any case, the journey of the quester-pilgrim, whether it be successful or unsuccessful, is the food on which great literature thrives.

A Bibliographical Note

The foregoing is, of course, only an introduction to literary analysis; but although necessarily incomplete, it may still allow one to begin to understand the nature and the meaning of literature and some of the ways to approach it. Here are a few important works on criticism—available in paperback—that may be of interest to readers of this book:

Booth, Wayne C., *The Rhetoric of Fiction,* Chicago, 1964.

Burke, Kenneth, *The Philosophy of Literary Form, Studies in Symbolic Action,* Vintage, 1957.

Daiches, David, *Critical Approaches to Literature,* Norton, 1956.

———, *A Study of Literature for Readers on Critics,* Norton, 1964.

Frye, Northrop, *Anatomy of Criticism, Four Essays,* Atheneum, 1965.

Hyman, Stanley Edgar, *The Armed Vision, A Study in the Methods of Modern Literary Criticism,* Vintage, 1955.

Prescott, Frederick Clarke, *The Poetic Mind,* Great Seal, 1959.

Richards, I. A., *Practical Criticism,* Harvest, 1929.

———, *Principles of Literary Criticism,* Harvest, 1925.

Wimsatt, W. K., Jr., *The Verbal Icon, Studies in the Meaning of Poetry,* Noonday, 1960.